DATE DUE

GAYLORD			PRINTED IN U.S.A.

THE NEW WOLVES

OTHER BOOKS BY RICK BASS

THE NEW WOLVES

RICK BASS

The Lyons Press

Printed in the United States of America
Printed on recycled paper

Sections of this book first appeared in *Audubon* magazine in
slightly different form.

A portion of the proceeds from the sales of this book will go
to Round River, a nonprofit, tax-exempt ecological research
and education organization. You can write to Round River at:
4301 Emigration Canyon, Salt Lake City, UT 84108.

10 9 8 7 6 5 4 3 2 1

FIRST EDITION

Excerpt from Cormac McCarthy's *Cities of the Plain*, copyright © 1998
by Cormac McCarthy, published by Alfred A. Knopf, Inc., is reprinted
by permission of International Creative Management, Inc.

Library of Congress Cataloging-in-Publication Data
Bass, Rick, 1958–
    The new wolves / Rick Bass.
        p.   cm.
    Includes index.
    ISBN 1-55821-697-9 (cloth).—ISBN 1-55821-773-8 (limited ed.)
    1. Mexican wolf—Southwest, New.   2. Wildlife reintroduction—
    Southwest, New.   I. Title.
QL737.C22B365   1998
599.773—dc21   98-36557
                                                                   CIP
Also published in a slipcased limited edition of two hundred and fifty copies.

For Mary Katherine and Lowry

CONTENTS

ACKNOWLEDGMENTS

It astounds me how many people have been involved for so long in what appears on the surface to be a most simple project: releasing eleven captive wolves into the mountains of Arizona. The people I became involved with during the course of this project represent only a tiny wedge of the total ongoing effort; but I am grateful for the time and energy of those few profiled in this book, and hope that they are somewhat representative of so many others, who, like the wolves themselves, may not have been glimpsed in this outing.

I'm grateful to Dave Parsons and Wendy Brown, of the United States Fish and Wildlife Service, for their sustained and diligent attention to the wolves—always operating in that thin space between passion, policy, and science. I'm grateful to the Turner Endangered Species Fund, Tom and Linda Savage, Jay Nochta, Keith Rutz, and all the other wolf volunteers. I'm grateful to PAWS (Protect Arizona's Wolves) not only for dreaming the idea of the return of Mexican wolves, but for following up on the dream with the hard work that lies beyond dreams; to Dave Foreman, Dennis Parker, and Jerry Scoville; to my agent, Bob Dattila.

I'm very grateful to my wife, Elizabeth Hughes Bass, for the illustrations, and to my editor on this project, Lilly Golden, to her assistant, Juliette Tritaris, and to Roger Cohn and the work he did as an editor while at *Audubon* magazine. David Brown's excellent book *The Wolf in the Southwest: The Making of an Endangered Species* (The University of Arizona Press) remains a classic source of information, and I'm grateful for it. I'm grateful to my typist, Angi Young, and to Trent Alvey and Carl Trujillo for their map of wolf distributions. I'm grateful to the ranchers Will and Sue Holder, and finally and especially to Dennis Sizemore and Round River Conservation Studies, and the Round River students, who continue, each year, to summon and nurture hope in all landscapes.

PREFACE

My family and I would see them hanging vertical from the corner post of the barbed-wire fence every Sunday, on our way to church; the freshly trapped red wolves, at the place we called Wolf Corner, on the outskirts of Houston. Sometimes there would be an assemblage of buff-colored coyotes flanking the larger red wolves, like angels aiding in the wolf's ascent. Sometimes there wouldn't be anything hanging from the fence, but they were there often enough to make the trip exciting for a seven-year-old boy, and it was always the highlight of the day: craning my neck to see, each Sunday, if anything new hung withering from Wolf Corner, at the edge of the rancher's property.

That was in the early 1960s. Gradually, through the years, the sightings of those vertical fence-hung pelts grew rarer and rarer, until finally we stopped looking for them, understanding that there were no more; and then the rangeland itself vanished, making way for a strip mall, a gas station, a florist's shop, and a James' Coney Island.

These were the kinds of stories the old geezers from my grandfather's and great-grandfather's era told, sitting around in rocking chairs, flapping their gums about the bygone days when they'd seen buffalo, or black bears in the Texas hill country, or mountain lions, or ocelots, or, once, a jaguar. And as a boy I confess that there was for me during the telling and retelling of such stories some implicit judgment on my part, unfair but present nonetheless, that the old-timers had somehow not been worthy of such wild treasury, which was the reason it had all gone away: the old farts had not been appreciative enough. I believed they must either have taken such wonders for granted, or never cared, so that by the time it was realized those creatures were vanishing, it was too late: the groove was already cut, and the lost species had disappeared down into that crevice.

And what matter? For then the oldsters followed them down into that same groove, also vanishing—though the oldsters left behind their legion spawn, *us*, while the wolves and grizzlies and condors and buffalo left nothing but thin scent and faint memories—distant echoes, distant tales.

I never intended, or believed, that one day I too would be telling such stories of loss—telling them with that same slightly unwitting sense of dumbfoundment: relating how a thing that was once wonderful and common came to exist no more. But already I have inherited my own stories, and so quickly—in such a short span of time. The last supposed Colorado grizzly was killed while I was in college. The last red wolf vanished from the Texas Gulf Coast around that same time. The last few Mexican wolves, or lobos, were gathered up and put in zoos, also during this period—the late 1970s. Ditto, as they say, for the condors, as our ecological impoverishment tracked all manner of downward spirals. At times it seemed possible, and still does, that one might run the risk of actually becoming inured to the process, such myriad comings and goings, such leave-takings; of leopard frogs, for crying out loud, and horned lizards, and spiny soft-shelled turtles. These things were everywhere when I was a child, and now they're all listed as threatened or endangered, and I'm not even forty years old.

What might the next forty years bring? The vanishing of horses, or crows, or butterflies? What God, or gods, will summon their return, and step forward with mercy to aid not their prosperity, but their mere survival?

HISTORIC DISTRIBUTION OF
WOLVES OF NORTH AMERICA

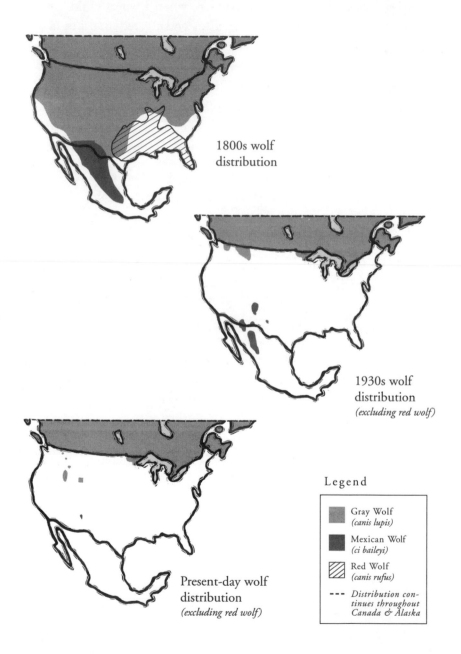

1800s wolf
distribution

1930s wolf
distribution
(excluding red wolf)

Present-day wolf
distribution
(excluding red wolf)

Legend

Gray Wolf
(canis lupis)

Mexican Wolf
(ci baileyi)

Red Wolf
(canis rufus)

--- *Distribution con-
tinues throughout
Canada & Alaska*

THE NEW WOLVES

Aint nothin to burn out there. I remember when you could have grassfires in this country.

I didnt mean I'd seen everything, John Grady said.

I know you didnt.

I just meant I'd seen things I'd as soon not of.

I know it. There's hard lessons in this world.

What's the hardest?

I dont know. Maybe it's just that when things are gone they're gone. They aint comin back.

Yessir.

They sat. After a while the old man said: The day after my fiftieth birthday in March of nineteen and seventeen I rode into the old headquarters at the Wilde well and there was six dead wolves hangin on the fence. I rode along the fence and ran my hand along em. I looked at their eyes. A government trapper had brought em in the night before. They'd been killed with poison baits. Strychnine. Whatever. Up in the Sacramentos. A week later he brought in four more. I aint heard a wolf in this country since. I suppose that's a good thing. They can be hell on stock. But I guess I was always what you might call superstitious. I know I damn sure wasnt religious. And it had always seemed to me that somethin can live and die but that the kind of thing that they were was always there. I didnt know you could poison that. I aint heard a wolf howl in thirty odd years. I dont know where you'd go to hear one. There may not be any such a place.

—from Cities of the Plain,
by Cormac McCarthy

DROUGHT

The American anthropologist W. W. Newcomb wrote: "The same sequences of events has occurred repeatedly in man's history; an invader with superior cultural equipment supplants and replaces a technologically inferior group. If the inferior culture survives it frequently does so in the marginal areas not coveted by the invader."

A map approximating where Mexican wolves *(Canis lupus baileyi)* last lived in the wild—or where they are still hanging on, if they are not extinct (the last confirmed sighting in the United States was in 1970; in Mexico, 1988)—looks almost exactly like the map of the distribution of the endangered Rocky Mountain gray wolf *(C. l. irremotus)* up along the border of Canada and northern Montana, before the wolves up there began to recover slowly: first on their own and then via helicopters, as wolves were trapped in British Columbia and relocated to Yellowstone National Park and Idaho.

The little fragments of map space that detailed the wolves' last strongholds—and then only the shadows, echoes, rumors, and memories of strongholds—is familiar for any vanishing species. We've seen the same map for a hundred different species. Always, they retreat to the places where man's machines cannot persecute them. And then, once isolated, they slowly vanish—the grand or magnificent ones, the ones that draw our attention. The specialized and unique ones disappear first: grizzly, buffalo, whooping crane, condor, wolverine, peregrine, lynx, woodland caribou, Sonoran pronghorn, desert pupfish—and on, and on.

The story repeats itself. It is as if some list exists and we must go down it, knocking them off one by one, as if in some macabre reverse version of Noah's Ark. *You*, off the ship, and *you*, and *you*.

It's been said—usually by resource-extraction industry representatives—that "extinction has always been natural and ongoing." This is true, though never has it proceeded at the current rate, which is a thousand times the pace of anything the world has ever seen. And in the past, as species were going extinct, other species were evolving in their place. But now as we scroll down our list of the fast-vanishing, what new and shiny species, what amazing replacements, are stepping forward to take the place of the departing?

What's amazing about the Mexican wolf—there are now about 175 in captivity, captive-bred from an initial population of only two or three family groups—is that wolves were once the most commonly distributed carnivore in the world, but are now among the rarest.

The Albuquerque Zoo has a handful of these treasures. You can walk right on in and look at them; you can peer over the adobe wall at these wolves—some of them old and stiff, all of them born in captivity (the original wild ones, captured down in Mexico, long ago blinked out)—and you can listen to the breeze flapping the palm fronds beneath which the wolves rest, on the other side of a moat. You can listen to the fluttering, flapping, city sound of pigeons, and to the five o'clock sound of downtown rush-hour traffic. You can look at those old wolves and wonder if they still have it in them or not.

There is a plan currently in progress (as mandated by federal law)—the Endangered Species Act, the closest thing we have to Noah's mandate—to bring Mexican wolves back from their "functional extinction" and to turn them back loose in the world.

There is a fair to even chance that if you watch the captive wolves, you'll decide they do not have it—wildness, and the ability to survive in this modern world. But if you stand there a while longer—watching nothing, or watching one of them sleep, dozing like, well, you hate to think it, like nothing more than a dog—until a raven drifts by, and utters a single short hoarse *croak*, and the wolf lifts its head and fixes burning yellow eyes on the sky in that direction with an intensity, a focus, for such a long period of time that all other city sounds fade for you and you are only watching that wolf's eyes watch the sky, you will begin to change your mind again and think, *Well, maybe they might make it after all.*

What is the Mexican wolf? Certainly in the wild it is a mystery. While the Rocky Mountain gray wolf often seems an enigma to our perception of landscape—sometimes bold, appearing right at the side of a highway, and other times moving deep into whatever traces of backcountry or wilderness can still be found—the Mexican wolf is instead an enigma to our perception of history.

Everything we know about Mexican wolves comes either from the behavior and measurements of wolves in zoos or, just as unreliably, from the records of the trappers who were chasing down, shooting, snaring, and poisoning a remnant population that had turned to preying on ranchers' livestock.

It seems to me safe to say that the behavior of a persecuted species, in the final days before its extinction from the wild, may not represent how that species would prefer to behave in the wild under more "normal" conditions.

We don't know what Mexican wolves did before our government started killing them in the late 1800s and early 1900s—which is, of course, when the big-time cattle empires collided with the landscape, having just finished eradicating the Indians and the buffalo. Even as the government and ranchers shot and skinned and tallied the last wolves, we were probably looking at the shadow of a thing rather than the thing itself.

David Brown's classic, *The Wolf in the Southwest*, contains observations by the first white settlers, who believed that the wolves occupying the Southwest lived only in the high mountains, where they preyed largely upon mule deer; though for every anecdote testifying to this, another can be found in which the wolves were encountered out on the grasslands.

The Spanish missionaries began losing livestock to wolves from the very beginning of their records—the mid-1500s. And Brown reported that in 1847 the Mormon battalion encountered the strange sight of a herd of cattle consisting almost entirely of bulls. A large cattle ranch in the area had abandoned its operations some years before, and evidently predators had killed the cows and calves and all but the largest bulls.

We know little else, beyond the general belief that wild, undisturbed Mexican wolves preferred the mountains before the cattle swept across the grassland and the wolves came down to avail themselves of the feast. (Buffalo were never much found in New Mexico and Arizona, due largely to the heat and aridity.)

We do know that Mexican wolves tend to be smaller than their northern cousins, and it's believed that their pack sizes are smaller. They do not appear to be shy about howling, and from anecdotal reports it seems possible that in the past they coexisted with coyotes more readily than do the larger gray wolves, which are somewhat renowned for killing dogs and coyotes, or for running them out of their territory.

The United States Fish and Wildlife Service describes a typical adult Mexican wolf as being about five and a half feet in total length—"German shepherd–size"—weighing between fifty and ninety pounds, and with a richly colored coat of buff, gray, rust, and black.

Their long forelegs are quite "wolfish," especially when they are trotting—but still, it is possible to mistake one for a coyote, if given only a glimpse.

We may not have the answers we want with regard to the science of wild Mexican wolves and their behavior—or any other kind of science—but perhaps this will become, among other things, a project in which we can begin learning, or relearning, which questions to ask. Perhaps we can even learn to ask them in time, before they become moot, irrelevant, gone and ghostly.

For example, a simple one: Which is richer and healthier: a world, a landscape, with only coyotes, or one with both wolves and coyotes?

Form follows function, and the earth has always desired wolves. While it's true that the skin of the earth is constantly sloughing and regenerating, mending and ripping, burning and growing, the mandate in the rocks themselves—which form soil, which yields vegetation, which sustains ungulates, which summon predators—is less capricious.

I do not believe that two lions, a bobcat, and three coyotes can be traded for one wolf. I believe that wolves simply cannot be erased; that they can be suppressed, even bent and altered, chained and shackled, or bred sideways into things-like-wolves that are not-quite-wolves—but that the earth needs wolves for balance, and that the wolves will again, sometime, somewhere, pop back up out of the rocks, to function amid the shape of the earth and its seasons.

When I think of the energy expended in trying to keep wolves pressed back down into the rocks, like ghost fossils, I grow uneasy. I consider the convulsive, shifting forces of volcanoes and plate tectonics. Yes, we can keep them down for a while, but at what cost? As we press down one tremble, one vibration on the earth's crust, what upwelling occurs behind us to take the place of wolves?

Cows is one answer that comes immediately to mind: the ponderous hooved weight of hundreds of thousands of cows pinning down the earth's crust and keeping the wolves trapped beneath that crust, though not for much longer now. The cows have been overgrazing the Southwest since they came to this region only four hundred years ago, and now the desert on which those descendant cattle tread is so thin that they are literally punching through it in places, while in other places—along the ephemeral seeps and springs of the riparian areas—the erosion is scouring and cutting gullies deeper and deeper into the soil, down through new soil and back into older soil, carrying the earth away in great salty gouts and deltas, cutting down to sun-heated bedrock. How can wolves not someday return from out of that bedrock? How can the cattle's overgrazing *not* summon them, and just in time?

Make no mistake about it: despite the nearly identical shapes on the map—the shape of the core of remaining wolf country up on our Canadian border, which so closely resembles the map of remaining wolf country down on our Mexican border—the gray wolf and the Mexican wolf are not the same subspecies, and as such may not play out their recovery in the same manner—no more than a stringed instrument symphony can sound like an orchestra of horns. I would love nothing more than to be wrong, and environmentalism—especially the twenty-first-century mandate of environmental restoration—cannot afford the luxury of pessimism, but the story of the recovery of wolves up in the north country such as Yellowstone has a lot of cushy factors going for it. Snow, for one, and an almost alarming abundance of prey. The wolves up there have a huge advantage in winter, moving across the deep snow so much more easily than their prey, and with the prey concentrating in large, predator-friendly herds in the winter.

Down south, when they come back, the Mexican wolves will be treading across rocks and stones, through thorns and thistles, which will be tough on their captivity-softened feet. Winter's opposite—the droughts of summer—might concentrate game in herds along the riparian areas (where wolves are most needed, to help stop or check the continued erosion in these areas), though that's also where people and their livestock might be. And it's true that the wolves survived down in this country for at least three million years before cows got here—but still, it's awfully damn hot down here, and that's another stress, intangible but real, that could make recovery tougher for the Mexican wolves than it is for those in the ongoing recovery in the northern Rockies.

To put it more simply—to cut to the base of my concerns—I believe that the land upon which the Mexican wolves will be asked to recover is in far worse shape and has been more abused than the lands up north in snow country. The phrase *give a dog a bone* comes to mind. Up north, we "gave" those wolves whole carcasses; down south, the land to which we're asking them to return is in many places the metaphorical equivalent of a scrap of withered hide.

And yet what do we really know of the earth's rhythms—the patterns and cycles of any scale beyond our own? Is it chance or fate that the wolves will be released in a relatively wet, lush, El Niño year? There's a fair chance that the "unnatural" rainfall patterns in the desert Southwest might give a temporary boost to the wolves' prey populations, which might—might—then be of some help to these newfound wolves. We don't know. The El Niño weather pattern in all its severity certainly wasn't factored into the proposed reintroduction. But here it is. The shadow of one thing—unknowable, unplannable—over the shadow of another unknowable, unplannable thing, the wolves themselves.

In many respects the recovery of Mexican wolves in the Southwest is currently taking the shape and function of the animal itself: smaller, less noticeable—not quite traveling at night and flying beneath radar, but certainly not bombing along with the high profile of, say, the Yellowstone airlifts. Perhaps things will go as relatively smoothly as they did in Yellowstone—the public and the media will yawn and say, "Ho-hum, another wolf reintro"—though perhaps, too, the land down here will shape and sculpt the recovery into something different.

I love the deep forests and snowy mountains—they seem to fit some space within me—and so perhaps it is totally my per-

sonal paranoia expressing itself when I imagine wolves on sun-
hot rocks in 115-degree temperatures, paws bleeding, existing on
lizards and the last decade's cow dung, gathered in one last small
pack and glaring at one another, panting, heavy radio collars
around their necks, wishing mightily they were back in the St.
Louis Zoo. But wolves possess what biologists call a "plasticity,"
meaning, among other things, that they've been here a hell of a
lot longer than we have. As long as we don't start killing them
again, there's a chance they can recover.

Perhaps it's only my blood's unfamiliarity with the earth's
language down in this part of the world that causes me such concern for the wolves. I'm more comfortable with the language of
wolverines, larch trees, spruce, marten.

Some of the words down in this "new" (to us) wolf country are similar to the north country, however. The Southwest's
jaguar is only a slightly different expression for the northern
Rockies' mountain lions (which are also found in the Southwest), just as the Mexican spotted owl is a slightly different
articulation of the north country's great gray owl. There are
familiar overlaps, too—ground squirrels, coyotes, mule deer,
whitetails, goshawks.

There are swells and uplifts in the Southwest whose elevations gain the ecology of valleys near my home in the north—
Ponderosa pines, and spruce and firs—but there are also strange
new words that form sentences almost unintelligible to me—
sweetly mysterious sentences and relationships that are still
draped over the form of the injured desert landscape: feral horse,
Gila chub, Gila monster, Gila spring snail; jaguarundi, javelina,
kit fox, Mexican long-nosed bat, ocelot, ringtail, water shrew.

And the vegetation—entire libraries of mystery! Arizona walnut, black grama grass, blue grama grass, creosote bush, Emory oak, Gambel oak, gray oak, honey mesquite; jojoba, sycamore, Texas madrona, sand sage.

We all have to make our living somewhere and some way, but it seems like tough country for a wolf. It is not the country it was when they last departed it.

The structural diversity in riparian areas is in senescence, chiefly because of a lack of recruitment among narrowleaf cottonwoods, Fremont cottonwoods, and Arizona sycamores, whose increasing absence is due largely to overgrazing by livestock. Without some sort of correction, soon even the old trees will disappear, leaving behind no structural diversity along the rivers: a sight as startling, perhaps, to the blood memory of the returning wolves as would be that of the mountains themselves leveled since the wolves' last forays into this country.

There has been a huge change, too, in the fire ecology of the region. The old grasslands have been invaded by seemingly endless swarms of piñon pine and juniper.

The native elk—Merriam's elk—has completely disappeared (hunted into extinction here) and since been replaced (via human management) by the Rocky Mountain elk: the same biological language, at least, though in a different dialect.

I wonder how long it will take them to learn the new language, and if they will tell the old stories or fashion new ones.

The new stories will have the old shapes, however, even if the words are different, because the tools used in the sculpting will be the same as they have always been: wind, gravity, rain, snow, rock, predation, speed, flight, power, endurance, intelligence, sight, taste, voice, scent, hearing, fire, ice. . .

Under the requirements of the Endangered Species Act, we-the-people are required to do all we can to help restore this subspecies, though we are doing so with relative timidity. Under a provision within the act, the released captive wolves will be classified as an "experimental" population, which means, among other things, that ranchers or anyone else whose livestock is harassed by the wolves can harass the wolves right back—can even kill them. It was under a similar experimental status that gray wolves were captured in British Columbia and shipped down to Idaho and Yellowstone National Park for reintroduction there. That process was ruled illegal late in 1997 because in granting experimental status to gray wolves in the area, the gray wolves that were already recolonizing the region naturally were stripped of the full protection of the Endangered Species Act and "downgraded" to experimental.

The wolves brought in from Canada might now have to be killed by the government, since recapturing them all and sending them back to Canada could prove impossible. The judge did offer extreme regret at his ruling, and his decision is being vigorously appealed. It's not thought that the ruling will affect the Mexican wolves' experimental status, because there seems to be a nil chance of any wild Mexican wolves remaining in the world to be negatively affected by such a downgrading.

Here, roughly, is how the reintroduction process is designed to take place:

The plan calls for the wolves to be kept in a kind of halfway house for at least a year to help them develop the kinds of behavior they will need to survive in the wild. Through 1997, these wolves were located at a captive-breeding facility on the Sevilleta National Wildlife Refuge, near Truth or Consequences, New Mexico. Three pairs of wolves—some with pups—will be selected initially and transported to three different temporary enclosures in the Apache National Forest of eastern Arizona, in the Blue Range, where they will live for a couple of months, being fed frozen deer and elk carcasses. Then in the spring, after the paired adult wolves have mated or at least bonded (wolves typically breed in late January or early February; pups are born sixty-three days later) and when their observers feel the wolves are ready, the gates will be opened. The wolves will leave their pens to venture out into the forest in what's known as a "soft release."

Then, we hope, the wolves will dig a den, give birth to pups—wild pups—and settle in to the countryside.

The three adult pairs—one for each release site—will be selected by their keepers for release based on a variety of criteria. They will not be genetically rare or unique among the captives, so that if they are killed they won't represent an extraordinary blow to the diversity of captive stock on hand. They will also be evaluated for various "human-avoidance" tendencies—general wariness—as well as for reproductive ability and an affinity for den digging, which should help keep them out of sight and increase the pups' (if there are any) chances of survival.

One of the most elemental maxims of wildlife management teaches that the prey controls the predator, rather than the other way around. The higher you sit atop the food or energy pyramid, the more dependent you are on all the factors below you. Still, it's a little basic to say that deer or elk control wolves as grass and forbs control deer, elk, or cows, as moisture and sunlight control grass and forbs—working down the flanks of that broad pyramid, back to the soil and then the bedrock, at which point the rot of all that's above conspires to bring blossoming new life. (And then up the pyramid life climbs once more—Kuenzler hedgeling cactus, night-blooming cereus, White Sands pupfish, Apache trout, southwestern willow flycatcher, Texas horned lizard, coatimundi, Mexican grizzly. . . .)

This is too basic because there are also relationships within the pyramid or, if you prefer, within the matrix. The shape is fluid, shifting and adjusting. Seen from a great remove in either time or distance, the distributions of energy resemble an inverted tornado—the famous pyramidal food chain—but rest assured that the closer you get, the less this is so. At any given moment in the center of the moil, a wolf has a deer by the throat, but nothing has yet been ceded, no energy yet surrendered or conquered and captured, and the two are rolling around and wrestling, blood in the sand, eyes bright in fury, and the deer is giving—in the moment—as good as it is getting, kicking and lunging and grunting, stabbing with its antlers. . . .

The prey, even in death, controls the predator by virtue of its lower, more stable position in the food chain. If the wolf or other predator is "too" successful, and consumes "too" much energy, the base will sag or collapse, bringing low population numbers of prey, and lean times. The predator will have to bide its time and wait for the prey to recover.

Waiting does not seem to us like a form of dominance.

In this respect the prey controls the predator; *everything* controls the predator—grass, sunlight, moisture. . . .

We know this, and we know also that predator and prey shape and sculpt one another, within that vortex. A common perception is that it's the predator that does all the carving—think of the oft-quoted line by the poet Robinson Jeffers, "What but the fine tooth of the wolf has whittled the fleet limbs of the antelope?"

Inside the moil, however, the relationships bend back on themselves, reciprocating, like Paul Bunyan's not-so-mythical Round River, which kept flowing back into itself. The Spanish philosopher José Ortega y Gasset wrote, in his book *Meditations on Hunting* that perhaps one of the reasons we hunt certain animals such as deer and quail, ducks and elk, is that there is "a relationship that certain animals impose on man, to the point where not trying to hunt them demands the intervention of our deliberate will." Thomas McIntyre addresses Gasset's writing in his book *Dreaming the Lion:*

> "According to Gasset, animals thought of as game are not hunted by chance, but because in the instinctive depths of their natures they have already foreseen the hunter (before he even enters the woods), and have, therefore, been shaped to be alert, suspicious and evasive. (Their shape, in turn, is what has molded our own—our forms, even the hard wiring of our brains, having been created for the function of hunting game animals.) And again according to the philosopher, the only adequate response to a being that lives obsessed with avoiding capture is to try to catch it."

Which brings me again—in the desert and in the Southwest—to cows.

By all accounts the wolves ate the hell out of cows. Scientists point out that it certainly wasn't all the wolves' "fault." It's believed by some, for instance, that the ranchers' and government's strychnine poisoning campaigns hurt, rather than helped, their goals of reducing or eliminating livestock predation. In the poisoning program, the ranchers and government trappers injected strychnine into any dead animal they found, whether it had been killed by wolves or not. According to biologist Jerry Scoville, this may have helped give rise to "socially retarded animals": wolves that, in order to survive, learned they had to kill their prey, eat once, then move on and kill again rather than return to a carcass—whether wild prey or livestock—and also to avoid feeding on any found carrion.

Brown reported that participants in John Bartlett's 1849–1851 survey of the U.S.–Mexico border observed Mexican ranchers lacing fresh livestock kills with strychnine. And in 1893 (following two years of intense drought, in conjunction with severe overstocking of livestock), the cattle industry in the Southwest collapsed. The dead and dying cattle (50–75 percent of the population) tempted more wolves down from the mountains. States passed the Territorial Bounty Act, which paid bounties of between ten and fifty dollars per kill. The wolves were hunted with traps, rifles, hounds, and poison. In 1907 the U.S. Forest Service joined in on the wolf exterminating. (In the first year, over 350 wolves were killed in the national forests of Arizona and New Mexico.)

The Predatory Animal and Rodent Control (PARC) branch of the U.S. Bureau of Biological Survey was formed in 1916—the predecessor to the Animal Damage Control program, which continues to be funded to this day—and these government hunters and trappers continued their war on wolves of all ages.

The ranchers pressured ever harder for the politicians, which is to say the government, to keep killing the wolves—every last one of them, or so it is widely believed—so that once again we can say, with accuracy, that the cows controlled the wolves, shaped them into near-extinction. And now that the cattle have eaten all of their "prey," which is the grass, grazing on the vast public lands in the Southwest is nearing its own extinction—the grass, or lack of it, controlling the grazers.

The wolves used familiar, traditional runways, which facilitated trapping, and so dependent had they become on the land's excess of livestock that a ranger or government-funded trapper had only to find a cow carcass and sprinkle poison into it, then come back in a day or two to find a ring of dead and dying wolves radiating outward.

By 1905 wolves were already scarce in the Southwest, but still the government kept pouring hate onto the land.

By 1925, Mexican wolves were mostly gone from the United States, with the exception of a few holdouts here and there in the most isolated regions; still, they kept crossing over from Mexico. Brown reported that there was one crossing between the Guadalupe and Peloncillo Mountains that was utilized by so many wolves that the PARC hoped to construct a border fence to keep them out. There is a curious report from 1937 by J. C. Gatlin that indicates wolf populations were increasing in Mexico, even as U.S. cattle interests were abandoning the region.

By 1950, however, even the wolves in Mexico were disappearing. Land reform by the Cárdenas administration—which broke up ranches into smaller fragments with more and more farmers and ranchers occupying smaller properties and coming more in contact with the wolves, as well as leading to an increase in overgrazing—helped diminish the number of wolves in Mexico, as did the creation of a new poison: Compound 1080, which was slow-acting but lethal, and selective to canids.

"Coyote-getters" were also placed in the field during this time, and were successful in helping decimate entire packs of the more social wolves, which tended to group together more than coyotes. In a 1969 edition of the journal *Wildlife Management Techniques*, T. E. Anderson describes the workings of a "coyote-getter":

> "It is a mechanical device which expels sodium cyanide and consists of a shell holder wrapped with fur, cloth, wool, or steel wool; a firing unit; a .38 cal. shell containing the sodium cyanide; and a 5–7 inch hollow stake. The stake is driven into the ground, the firing unit is cocked and placed in the stake and the shell holder containing the cyanide shell is screwed onto the firing unit. A fetid bait, usually made of fish, brains, or blood, is carefully spread on the shell holder. The cartridge fires when the animal pulls up the shell holder and the cyanide is blown into the animal's mouth."

After about fifteen seconds of what we can assume must be agony, the animal lapses into a coma, then dies.

By 1960 there were only the rarest sightings of Mexican wolves. (At this point, Yellowstone's wolves had been gone for several decades.) Each wolf found trapped or poisoned in the Southwest was thought to be surely "the last Mexican wolf." And finally, in 1970, the last one *was* killed in West Texas, and the last one in Arizona in 1975, and in New Mexico in 1976.

It occurs to me that the big-time cattle industry was doomed from the beginning, as is anything that begins with a biological inaccuracy. What believer in justice could possibly expect a system to succeed that had as the cornerstone of its success genocide? As the Indians were being killed off early in this country's white history, Ghost Dances told of the land's former inhabitants—the wolves, buffalo, and grizzlies—returning to the land. The prophecies did not mean this would happen immediately, but often spoke of this rebirth occurring in the seventh generation, which would be, by some counts, the one upon us now.

Another biological inaccuracy upon which our present culture was built, especially in the Great Plains, was the error of replacing the free-ranging bison herds with strung-and-fenced cattle herds—a substitution so controlled and static as to be almost mechanized.

The units of animal mass were nearly the same. In his book *Grassland*, Richard Manning wrote that after all was said and done—all the massacres, scalpings, and butchery; all the postholes dug and fence strung; all the wars and protests of the last 150 years; all the irrigation diversions, feedlots, and corrals; all the millions of gallons of human blood sprayed across the American West in great splashing red gouts, like paint across a canvas—we succeeded in achieving a minor transformation, a temporary alteration to the face of the land, like little gods or devils: replacing fifty to a hundred million bison with ninety-five million cattle.

But biologically, the cattle do not fit this land, and a thing that is begun wrong can rarely end well. The culture before ours, wrote historian Richard White, "linked the success of human endeavors to the biological success" of the animals, but the next dominant cycle of civilization—the Europeans— believed they "could see their own commercial success as tied to the virtual destruction of entire species."

White reported, "If a roof had been built over the southern plains in the early 1870s . . . it would have been 'one vast charnel-house.' During the fall of 1873 the corpses, [bison] stinking and rotting in the sun, lay in a line for forty miles along the north bank of the Arkansas River [in Colorado and Kansas]. William Blackmore, an English traveler, counted sixty-seven bodies in a space not covering four acres."

And beneath these bison, only half an inch below them in the soil—and above them, too, in the coming years—lay the bones and blood and cultures of the Sioux, Apache, Comanche, Navajo, Ute, Pawnee, stacked crossways and diagonal among and between the bones of bison and grassland like a latticework of timbers, whose rotting and splintering can no longer support that which rests so heavily above it; rot settling in now atop rot.

There was for a while—before the Indians were all killed or caged—a type of wild livestock, the longhorn or "Spanish or Mexican cattle," that rivaled the buffalo for durability, but that could tolerate the heat better and as such could prosper much farther south. Rangy, lean, sway backed, and ferocious, they might not fare well in today's market of marbled, fatty beef and the demands for highest maximum biomass yields per animal unit. But before the fencing and domesticating and crossbreeding of cattle in the Southwest, the longhorns held their own. The steers in particular possessed tremendous horns—one individual's

measured nine feet across—and often whenever the wolves considered harassing them, the longhorns would form an impene-
trable defensive circle, sweeping horns facing out, as did the
buffalo farther north under similar circumstances.

(Sometimes a wolf might catch a young longhorn out on
the range and, in biting at its flanks, castrate the animal; the
calves who survived such excisions went on to become steers of
prodigious size, growing horns far larger, and attaining more mass,
than had they not been "cut." It is almost as if in failing to bring
that male calf down, the wolves had instead given rise to something near mythic, a steer they would never again be able to
harass or injure.)

The longhorns were creatures of the open range, as wild
as the other game in the country, and able to be herded in great
numbers only through much vigilance on the part of the cowboys. So wild were stray individuals that they were hunted for
food as if they were deer, and were considered, according to the
Texas folklorist J. Frank Dobie, to be "the peer of the bison and
grizzly bear"—a part of the natural history of the Southwest, one
in which Texas became the primary nursery for the breed.

They were not prone to the dreaded screwworm that
later preyed so heavily on domestic cattle; with their thick tails
they could keep the flies swished away, and when wounded they
would stand in a river, like a deer or other wild creature, to
keep flies from ravaging the wound. The longhorns were
deemed by some cowboys to be more dangerous than grizzlies,
and—again as related by Dobie—"a wounded bull has been
known to hunt for his enemy by scent, trailing him on the
ground like a bear."

Dobie wrote, "The longhorns were probably more effective against lobos than were the buffaloes. John Williams, who has for many years worked in the great lobo-infested Babicora range of western Chihuahua . . . has told me that he once came upon three lobos pulling down a calf; about the time he arrived on the scene, seven Mexican cows [longhorns] arrived also and chased the wolves into the breaks. The Mexican cattle throve and increased and multiplied surrounded by lobos, but the Herefords had to be protected; man had to kill the lobos off in order for the whitefaces to maintain existence."

When the longhorns could be gathered up and driven, it was theorized that the heat from the herd's mass attracted lightning. (Such was the radiant heat from a large herd that a cowboy's face would be blistered on whichever side of the herd he'd ridden by the day's end.) Their great horns also seemed to attract electricity, so that lightning and ground-electricity would bounce around from horn to horn throughout the herd—a phantasmagoric buzzing blue circuitry. The cracking of the cowboys' whips and the twitching of the cattle's tails also emitted sparkling "snakes of fire."

Understandably, such a phenomenon—raw electricity flowing through the sky, through the land, and through the herd itself—tended to spook the longhorns, and would cause them to stampede; as would the odor of wolves, or any other predator.

"Here was a great herd," wrote Dobie, "any antlered creature of which would have chased the biggest lobo of North America and, if able to catch him, would have gored him to death; yet the sharp smell of a coyote cub coming unexpectantly to a certain steer might startle him and the startlement be instantly translated into mob panic."

The bulls would often fight at night, clashing and grunting and rearing, pawing huge troughs of soil and slamming their horns together and sometimes flipping and even goring one another. The wolves—the same wolves that rest now caged behind bars, or at least their murmuring bloodlines—would gather at the starlit perimeters of such fights and serenade the battles with their howls, hoping for one of the bulls to kill the other.

Beyond the wolves' perimeter would gather the little coyotes, whose yaps and shrieks would mix with the wolves' deep howls and the bulls' roars to fill the whole prairie with sound, a symphony we no longer hear and can barely even imagine.

The cattle drivers called such battles "prayer-meetings" and would remark, somewhat casually, that the bulls were "testifying," and then would go back to eating their beans, or staring at their fire, or whatever it was they were doing, for there was nothing that could be done out on the open range when two longhorn bulls got that way: nothing to do but wait it out and see which one would win.

There is yet another biological inaccuracy or error that the new wolves will be forced to deal with upon their return: the absence of fire. The Indians used it to rejuvenate the grasslands and to keep these lands from being swarmed over with brush and other woody debris. They called fire the "red buffalo," and between the migrations of bison and the creeping, crawling fertilization of the fires—with the wolves and the Indians follow-ing the bison, pushing them here and there, so that the land was always lightly grazed, *stimulated*—the land was alive and supple, back then, with a pulse, an electricity.

Fire has been gone from the country for almost as long as the wolves, Indians, and buffalo, and in too many places now rather than the pulse of grass bending in the wind there is a static, tangled clot—a latticework—of dried brush and timber resting atop powdery soil and sand.

The law of the land—of rock and earth—says that the wolves will be back; and that the bison will be back, too, or a thing more like bison; and fire will be back also. And from all this, surely, will come a human culture or cultures more like those old ones—less fragmented, more connected to, and more grateful for, the land's resources.

The law of Congress also calls for the wolves and other wild treasures to return. And despite the political bends and alterations affixed to the law before it is implemented, the wolves will be coming back. The only question lies within the condi-tions our political system will impose upon those wolves—where they will be tolerated, where they will be supported or encour-aged, and where they will be persecuted; how closely our altered law will fit that of the land.

It is a fact that a century's worth of wolves returning to this hammered land will no longer have as much impact upon cattle as one hour of international traders' commodity brokering. The ranchers know this as well as anyone, and many of the ranchers will tell you that they hold nothing personal against the

wolf, and even identify with it, in some respects. But the ranchers feel economically and culturally marginalized, pushed to the
edge of existence, to the edge of survivability, and then beyond.
The ranchers will tell you, perhaps 99.9 percent of them—small
in number but huge in put-upon, abused, wronged, even martyred
fury—that it is the federal government's intervention into matters about which it knows nothing and in which it has no stake,
no understanding or *compassion*, that they resent: not *Canis lupus
baileyi*.

What the ranchers will not tell you, however, is that the
land to which the small handful of wolves will be returned is in
ragged, horrific shape. Rather than returning to the meat of the
land, the wolves will now encounter, in most places, the land's
skeleton.

The ranchers will speak instead of the miraculous reju-
venating powers of the land; of how green pastures, health, vitality, and power are always only one rain away in the West. They
will tell you of the incredible speed with which the land heals.

I don't believe them. I don't think they're being untruth-
ful—only mistaken. I think they're remembering a younger land—
a younger soil, fifty, sixty years ago—and younger selves, too.

Perhaps fire is to the West what rain is to the East.

It's been a long drought, and it has everything, and nothing, to do with wolves.

THE
STUDENTS

There are six of them, as well as two instructors, using an old Forest Service cabin for their headquarters. The Round River Conservation Studies program, based in Salt Lake City, Utah, takes small groups of college students into the woods each year and teaches them field methods in ecology, conservation biology, and even some journalism and natural history literature, for college credit. (Other areas across the West where Round River students have been active are the British Columbia rain forest, the San Juan Mountains grizzly project in Colorado, and the Yaak Valley grizzly project in Montana.) The students spend twelve weeks in the field mapping vegetation types and, in the case of the Mexican wolf project, mapping prey densities—mule deer, Coues' white-tailed deer, javelinas, rabbits, elk (in the higher elevations)—as well as inventorying and describing other vital aspects of the ecosystem.

The students have been prowling the creek bottoms, taking note of springtime black-hawk nests, and interviewing individuals in the nearby ranching communities, talking to them about why they (the students) want wolves to return to this area, as well as learning about ranching, compiling community profiles, and attending town meetings.

The students' camp is over an hour from the nearest hard-surfaced road, an hour and a half from the nearest town. In some ways *they* are the locals, here in the heart of the Blue Mountains of southern Arizona, very near the New Mexico state line.

There once were wolves here. The old man who last lived in this cabin died from a grizzly mauling many years ago. It wasn't an Arizona grizzly that killed him—it was one of the last grizzlies down in Mexico, and the man didn't die immediately but came back to his cabin here along the creek and lingered for *years*, as I understand it, before dying ultimately of complications from his injuries. The story, even though it doesn't involve a Blue Range grizzly (they too were here, farther back in time), lends a certain air to the place, a certain moodiness and authority of the wild.

The Round River students—a different batch each semester—have been coming here for three years, helping lay the foundation and framework for the release of captive Mexican wolves. The decisions that get made about where the wolves are to be released will be based somewhat on biology and somewhat on politics—it depends on who you talk to as to the varying percentages of each—but in the meantime the students are traveling the side canyons and backcountry tirelessly, making notes and maps, and detailing the things they find. *Here is where the whitetail winter range appears to be—antlers everywhere; here is where we find much mountain lion sign, in the summer; here is where the javelina population seems densest. . . .*

Wild roses bloom in the courtyard outside the old cabin. Biology textbooks, as well as books of poetry, lie open all over the porch, pages shining brilliant white, almost glowing, in the spring sunlight that shafts down through the green leaves of giant cottonwoods. The river breeze stirs and rattles the leaves of the cottonwoods, and sometimes the pages in one of the books flip slowly, as if being read by an invisible reader.

All was not poetry and the intellect here a few short days ago; it's strange how many different layers and stories are laid across this land. Some of this story's participants have come to give something to the land, or to the story, while others have come to take. Just last week, prior to the arrival of the Round River students, there was an encampment of pig hunters/militia members living in the Forest Service cabin—unauthorized, unregulated, unpermitted, and uncontested—for several months. There was quite a crowd of them—men, women, and children—and from the accounts they left in the cabin's journal, they practiced paramilitary operations and shot javelinas. It appeared that they used the barn for an out-house—human feces lay scattered randomly and in great quantity throughout the barn—and they also left behind the hides and skulls and gleaming bones of whichever javelinas had been un-fortunate enough to cross their path. Basically, some folks who disliked the law and believed themselves beyond it found a place they liked and settled in. This is, again, not unlike the stories that have already been laid down across most of the arid West: outlaws, society's economic and cultural and religious refugees leaving the margins of their old lives to form new cores and centers else-where—the Mormons, the mountain men, the timber industry, miners, ranchers. . . . It reminds me of the arguments going on in science in the 1850s—Louis Agassiz holding that each of the stages of evolution was predestined by God, locked like an unread but already-written transcript within the earth, while Darwin was for-mulating that it was a much more savage affair, tooth-and-claw struggles going on in every living, breathing moment, and that the stories of life were in no way already written.

It's a dubious, circular argument—a question of scale and intricacy far beyond our understanding. The theologians could argue that evolution itself is already coded into the earth, that there can be no randomness, if you are aware of enough factors and plug them all into the equation; that all the variables, infi-nite in number, can conspire to produce only one outcome.

Who cares? Surely the truth lies not at the beginning or end of the circle but, as with most things, somewhere in between.

Nearly two hundred years of white history lies scratched loosely and in tiny type across this portion of the West, and the stories all seem to be told by the same teller. We have to wonder if again our lives and stories are like blankets waiting to be laid down across the surface of the land, shaped by the topography beneath; or—chasing our tails once more—does there exist in us certain genotypes and phenotypes, certain brands of people desiring certain topographies, so that we drift, or are restless, until we come to the one place that fits the curve of our brain, the curves of our body?

Do we happen to the land, or does the land happen to us?

Again, it is a question of scale. I think the land still happens to us. Perhaps not as dramatically as it once did—but I believe the land still shapes and influences us dramatically.

Anyway, the militia people had departed earlier in the week, leaving cryptic messages in the Forest Service journal dated by military time—"0900 hours," and so on—with most of the entries penned by one Captain Black Dog. And like a tide, the students have come sweeping in: vegetarians, poets, dreamers. All this change in one week! It might take the land ten thousand millennia to affect such a juxtaposition in one place—to turn a mountain into a sea, or an ocean into a mountain.

I cannot help but keep believing that—against whatever odds—wolves will make it back to this land because the land desires it; and that our own puny efforts to control, maneuver, or manage the timing and extent of this return will be the geologic equivalent of an infant who seizes a pen and scribbles for a moment on a piece of paper that already has writing on it.

This is not to say at all that we shouldn't make the attempt. The absence of wolves is clearly a biological wrong—a fragmentation, an injury—but it encourages me that we still have somewhat in us the urge to mend that wrong.

I do not expect the story to come as gracefully or easily or *hypothetically* upon the land as it does at our desks and in our offices and books of regulations. We still have so much to learn about wildness.

The students found a dead bobcat up the creek, collapsed by water's edge, dead from no apparent injuries. They performed a ceremony for the creature, a ritual, designed, like almost all rituals, to try and give ourselves rest and peace of mind: a thing done for our solace, rather than for the departed.

The country where the students are hanging out used to have a few cattle roaming through it, though the cattle have been taken off the land gradually over the last ten years because of drought conditions, and the ecological wreckage caused by overstocking. Earlier in the day, a Forest Service ranger had come out to visit with the students and spoke to them about the idea of perhaps turning herds of goats out onto the land, as a way of allowing the culture of ranching to remain somewhat in place, yet to allow some healing of the land to begin—or to at least begin to stanch the bleeding in places where the soil itself is now washing away like blood. (Eighty to ninety percent of all vertebrates in the Southwest spend part or all of their life in the riparian areas.)

I missed the lecture, but from the way the students described it, it would be a kind of goat fire: herds and packs of goats, maybe ten thousand goats, moving through the under-brush, browsing leaves and twigs—overbrowsing them, managed thus in an effort to make the invasive woody debris disappear—

and in the process spreading their shit pellets far and wide across the landscape, out of which, in theory, grasses could return.

The mechanical action of tens of thousands of little goat hooves, went the theory—as it was related to me—would help perforate and aerate what scant remaining soil there is, which has been rendered useless, compacted by the heavy cattle trudging back and forth across it seeking shade and forage and water.

The students said they listened politely, courteously, and tried to learn, but were impatient. They didn't want swarms of magic goats, bleating and squalling, bells tinkling, moving across the landscape—across their public lands. They wanted wolf music. They wanted to go straight to the matter in the most direct and forceful manner. *Bring the wolves back.* Then let the wolves do the writing—let the wolves sort things out.

I like it when the lines blur between students and teachers: when you're not sure who's doing the teaching.

THE
WOLVES

Maybe twenty-five or thirty of them still reside in Mexico, though there could just as easily be zero; no sign of them has been found now for ten years. Similarly, it's thought that zero remain in the United States in the wild—though who can say: there are rumors, and shadows behind rumors. Glimpses, and faint tracks, and an occasional wind-tossed sound like a howl, or the echo of a howl.

From what little is known about the natural history of wild Mexican wolves, they seem well suited to secrecy. Being smaller than other wolves is an evolutionary adaptation that gives them a larger surface-area-to-mass ratio and allows them to dissipate heat quickly.

Pack size in wolves can be related to any combination of a number of factors, but without question availability of prey is one of the most important of these, and generally speaking—there will be exceptions—the arid, rocky Southwest doesn't yield the same per-acre biomass of prey that the wetter regions farther north produce. Hence a southern wolf pack of equal size would have to range much farther than a northern pack—perhaps farther than physically possible, given caloric intake versus demands—or else the pack must break into smaller bands and packs. (Again the land answers these questions—stretches and pulls them almost like taffy.)

Another factor influencing the natural history of Mexican wolves is, of course, the type of prey available to them. Obviously, in a land of Coues' white-tailed deer, many of which might not weigh more than a single wolf, or javelinas, which, though fierce, weigh less—even one lone wolf could be success-ful. Will the Mexican wolves travel farther than gray wolves, in a more austere landscape, or will they not travel nearly as far —consisting (we theorize) of smaller pack sizes? *We don't know.*

Up north in snow country, where the prey is sometimes moose and elk, a larger pack size is required just for the sheer mechanics of hauling down so much runaway meat.

The lobo can weigh between fifty and ninety pounds as an adult. Even at the low end of this scale it'll be larger than almost any coyote in the same landscape, and at the high end there'll be no mistaking it: a ninety-pound wolf has the habit of looking twice its size.

Their fur coloration can vary but predictably contains the hues of the landscape: reds, oranges, silvers, buffs. Adults can stand twenty-six to thirty-two inches at the shoulder, and average between four and a half to five and a half feet in total (tail included) length.

Again, one of the wonderful, exciting, and alarming things about the reintroduction is that there was little "scientific research" done on the Mexican wolves back in the days when they lived in the wild. "The only field data," according to a U.S. Fish and Wildlife Service 1996 Draft Environmental Impact Statement (EIS), "came from a period of rapidly dwindling numbers when human activities had disrupted pack structures and natural prey populations."

There is so much we don't know—and for the first time that I can tell, the agencies in charge of the recovery seem willing to acknowledge that they, or we, don't know. It's going to be fresh. Maybe good, maybe bad, but fresh, exciting, vital. The released wolves might be drawn to the paved parking lots of Tucson. They might chase cattle. We hope they will go where wolves used to go. Their core areas, as best we can tell, seem to have been the higher-elevation Ponderosa pine forests and mixed piñon-oak woodlands—and it would seem they will follow the pattern of so many other large endangered mammals in this country, retreating to the interiors of remote, roadless places then further isolating themselves into the high country, or to the edge of the high country. But that's the thing about wolves—as about humans—and especially these Mexican wolves: nobody knows. Wolves have to go where the game is. The prey controls the predator.

They have to bring in the meat. They have to go out and get it.

How much?

The recovery's goal is modest: 100 wolves in the five-thousand-square-mile recovery area and 240 wolves in captivity, for use as breeding stock. (There were once tens, perhaps hundreds of thousands of Mexican wolves.) Computer modeling estimates tell us that a hundred wolves would kill prey totaling about 282,300 pounds per year: an undefinable smorgasbord of mule deer, elk, and Coues' white-tailed deer. What the computer can't analyze with as much confidence is what is called, delicately, "alternate prey use"—anything other than a deer or elk. This could be cottontails or javelinas, or it could be chickens and cows.

Another factor with which the computer programmers were not comfortable was the idea of "compensatory mortality." This refers to deer and elk killed and eaten (or scavenged) by the wolves when these deer or elk would have died from another cause at about the same time anyway.

I don't really want to get into all the numbers and assumptions—it would be too easy to spend time fretting over them when they're probably going to turn out differently anyway—but the computer's bottom line under the USF&WS plan is that fifteen years after the wolves are released, human hunters' deer kills might be reduced by between 6 and 17 percent; there might be a reduction in the human elk harvest of between 5 and 13 percent.

I'm a hunter, and these numbers don't bother me—wouldn't bother me if they occurred in my valley. No hunter considers him- or herself in the bottom 5 percent, or even the bottom 17 percent, in either skill or luck—we'd always figure it would be the other guy who didn't get a deer that year because of the wolves. We'd just hunt 5 percent harder, or 17 percent harder, and the intangible trade-offs—the "compensatory intangible benefits," as the feds might say—would be enormous.

To hear the wolves howling at night; to be hunting in a fuller, healthier ecosystem; to be able to observe the increased physical, genetic vigor of the herds, once wolves were among them—all of these things would be welcomed by the hunters I know. Some "road" hunters might disagree, though now an analyst would be looking at a subcategory of hunters, the "shooters"—but even then, so what? Let the "shooters" drive 5 percent farther to find their prey.

Or perhaps a couple hundred fewer deer might induce the shooters to park their trucks and get out and walk a short distance into the brush, into the mountains, and in so doing perhaps they would gain a connection to the landscape, and an awareness and respect for it that might otherwise be missing.

A lack of that kind of ecological awareness, or grounding, on the part of the general public is one of the things that got the wolves and the landscape in this trouble in the first place. It's easy to dramatize in the media the slashing teeth of wolf packs pulling down a couple hundred deer per year, as they have done for millennia; less outrageous, to the public's eye, are the grinding teeth of overstocked cattle herds standing around in one place, compacting the soil into hardpan and eating so much grass that hundreds or thousands of elk starve, or are never born in the first place. Surely the terrible teeth of cattle should be more horrifying to hunters than the teeth of wolves. Sixty years ago Aldo Leopold said this eloquently, and still we are not listening fully.

In his book *Gila: The Life and Death of an American River*, Gregory McNamee tells of the time Leopold killed a wolf and her pups, but then came to understand the intricate relationships among predator, prey, and landscape. McNamee wrote of Leopold:

> "The critical moment came . . . when he killed an old wolf in a valley along the San Francisco River. He and his companions fired round after round into the wolf and her pups, then scrambled down the embankment from which they had been shooting to tally up the score. As he recalled, 'We reached the old wolf in time to watch a fierce green fire dying in her eyes. . . . I was young then and full of trigger-itch; I thought that because fewer wolves meant more deer, no wolves would mean hunters' paradise. But after seeing the green fire die, I sensed that neither the wolf nor the mountain agreed with such a view. . . . The cowman who cleans his range of wolves does not realize that he is taking over the wolf's job of trimming the herd to fit the range. He has not learned to think like a mountain. Hence we have dustbowls, and rivers washing the future into the sea.' "

The wolves are coming, and certain things will happen as a result. Surely for them it will be as if they have awakened from a long sleep—a hibernation of sorts. There will be changes: some on a geologic scale, but others on the more visible and more dramatic scale of humans and our perceptions.

◆ ◆ ◆

How this southern subspecies fits into the wolf family tree is a matter of debate. Of course, it's possible that we've lost a vast sheet of wolf subspecies, and where the Mexican wolf fits into that history will remain a mystery.

The taxonomic preferences of lumpers and splitters are well known; though a crass stereotype, it could be generalized that lumpers are more the loose laissez-faire types of scientists who believe time and the landscape are going to work to sort and smooth things out (or erase them) anyway, while the splitters can be thought of, in this vein of stereotyping and caricature, as maniacal individuals of such intellectual prowess—able to discern and retain so much data—as to possess knowledge, through the naming and classification and then subclassification of every genetic blemish or aberration, of every individual act of nature; as if it all has a name and a category, and the mysteries of flux and evolution are like some prey floundering across the snow toward which they are always wolfishly drawn, seeking to pin down and control it with their naming and subnaming.

I'm a lumper.

It—lumping or splitting—seems to me to depend mostly upon your wiring within: how much you choose to see or consume in a single glance.

The reason this eternal scientific squabble or tension is of interest with regard to the Mexican wolves is that not everyone is sure of what we've got; even now, with all of the known wolves in captivity, they maintain a certain secrecy within. It's not the easiest thing in the world to say what a Mexican wolf *is*.

Back in the 1940s and '50s, scientists described (based on skull size and shape, mostly, as if it's the brain that responds most vividly—or with least variance—to the shapes and sculptings of the landscape) twenty-four subspecies of wolves in North America, five of which occurred in the southwestern United States and Mexico and could be properly called "lobos." Their names were *Canis lupus baileyi*, *C. l. mogollonensis*, *C. l. monstrabilis*, *C. l. nubilus*, and *C. l. youngi*.

Subsequent reclassifications tried to achieve some lumping and hence scientific workability. (Remember that the home ranges of these twenty-four subspecies, or however many there really were, tended to overlap dramatically, with all the zones of genetic mixing and integration you'd expect from a wide-ranging, highly social mammal.) The USF&WS Final EIS noted, with near-audible relief, "It should be noted that no individual taxonomist or publication has official or ruling status on questions of mammalian taxonomy."

The consensus, however, seems to be that the Mexican wolves we've got behind bars are *Canis lupus baileyi*, gotten from Mexico, and that this is the same subspecies that once occupied areas in Arizona, Texas, and New Mexico.

It seems like a big fuss to me. I'm convinced that you could take (if they weren't already extinct) *C. l. monstrabilis* ("the buffalo wolf") or *C. l. mogollonensis* or, hell, even *C. l. irremotus*, the northern Rocky Mountain gray wolf, and put them into the Southwest, then these particular mountains and rivers would sculpt that protoplasm, would bend those genes, into something very much resembling the "original" *C. l. baileyi* that now rests behind bars. It might just take an extra hundred thousand years.

To a lumper, the obsession with the categorization of extinct and shifting subspecies all seems to be a lot of more or less irrelevant nattering. Let's go with what we've got, the pragmatist will urge. And what other choice is there? But such abstract considerations of the scale of evolutionary change and the firm guiding hand of geology are useful in reflecting upon how utterly brutish, even malevolent, our own hand has been upon the land in this part of the world. We've damn near eradicated, in sixty or so years, that which took two million to create.

It can go so fast. As recently as 1980 a trapper, Roy McBride, who helped capture the last five known wild Mexican wolves down in Mexico for captive-breeding stock, estimated that "some fifty wolves may still inhabit Mexico." Computer simulations based on that estimate indicated that this suggested population of fifty remnant animals would have become extinct by 1994.

How can we be sure that a wolf planned for release is certified as being a Mexican wolf, rather than, say, a Canadian gray wolf, or a husky/coyote cross, or a Mexican wolf/dog hybrid?

Once again, state-of-the-art, or state-of-the-science, DNA analyses have been run on all the "candidate" wolves. Molecular "microsatellites" (within the DNA) are graphed and stripped under electron microscopes. The waverings, the bands, of darkness and light show up as genetic fingerprints, appearing beneath the microscope to the blurring eyes as broad valleys and high mountains—great vistas of time and space. The truth is revealed.

Of the 175-plus captive Mexican wolves, there are only three known lineages: the initial five wolves trapped by McBride in the period from 1977 to 1980; the "Ghost Ranch" lineage, kept at the Ghost Ranch Living Museum in northern New Mexico; and the Aragon lineage, from the Aragon Zoo in Mexico City.

So many, from so few. It seems remarkably biblical—a population of our future wolves springing back up out of almost nothing: dust and clay, water, mud. Perhaps the stories of creation and genesis will also be the models for stories of re-creation.

At the twenty-eight wolf-breeding facilities around the United States and Mexico (I envision them presently fragmented, like the incomplete sets of points in a connect-the-dots exercise) scientists are studying the genetics of each new pup, and the wolves' keepers are studying the characteristics of the individual animals, making notes as to which wolves possess those qualities—namely, that immeasurable *wildness*—best suited for a release back into the real world.

The gene for secrecy has not yet been pinpointed, so it is up to the wolves' keepers as much as the scientists. They make hunches and guesses, consult with the scientists, and trade males and females, trying not to disrupt too much the natural selection of alpha (dominant) wolves choosing to breed with one another, and yet trying also to avoid falling too far into that dreaded trap, the sinkhole or bottleneck of genetic inbreeding.

The wolf recovery experts have a word for such a thing: *redundancy*. They try to keep the genetic redundants—the strains, the types, they already have—away from each other. They try unlikely or uncommon pairings—hoping to inflate, rather than deflate and isolate, genetic variability. It's alarmingly like growing a crop.

And it's not like the wolves have got it made in the shade, hanging out in zoos. It's as if they still possess some back-

ground ferocity, which seems to be urging us to *Hurry, hurry.*
Early on in the captive-breeding process, one female wolf killed
another: an extremely discouraging setback to the genetic diversity of the "founding" population. Yet another wolf—a male
pup—was struck and killed by a bolt of lightning within his pen.

Believing as strongly as I do that the landscape has a guiding hand in carving and sculpting a species—in choosing or influencing, for instance, which wolves are alphas, which are omegas
(lone wolves), and so on, which genes get together when, as well
as which ones prosper while others fail—then it's of little or no
solace to me that the glimmerings of some genetic bar code indicate that we have a diverse and healthy batch of Mexican wolves
ready to cast back out into the world. The longer the wolves stay
in captivity—generation after generation after generation—the
more I worry that a thing, a wildness and a vitality, may be draining out of them; that no matter what variability the genetic maps
and sequencings indicate they have, it is an untested variability
and hence suspect, weaker, and less vital than one forged by the
landscape.

Or rather, I worry that it is precisely the landscape that *is*
shaping these wolves: that they are being formed and fashioned
and shaped by the landscape of iron bars, the fields of concrete,
generation after generation.

I worry that a thing—an invisible thing—is somehow
fading from them; and that once it begins leaving them, it can
go fast.

There are so many questions, so many layers. It is as if we
have taken a knife to a tightly woven rope of many braids, and

are now trying to repair it to how it was. Some magic will need to be involved; the rope will have to miraculously do some of the healing and reattaching itself.

Do we shake the wolves loose into the world as if out of a burlap bag—a "hard release"? Or do we use a "soft release," in which they're kept in an enclosure out in the woods, breeding perhaps and even raising pups? How do we teach them to hunt, and to hunt the most difficult thing of all—wild game—rather than the easiest, which is livestock? Captive-raised red wolves that were released into the southeastern United States learned to hunt on their own, so we know it can be done.

Will they pack up or break into smaller, more disparate units? Will they breed with coyotes? Will their skulls lengthen and broaden to hold new data? Or do the old secrets, old data, still reside within them, waiting to be summoned once again?

We are all creatures of landscape. We are creatures of our past, and the larger the past is, the harder it is to tell new stories.

I think the new wolves will be pretty much like the old wolves, at first. But we have so altered the landscape since they were last upon it that perhaps this will not be the case.

Again, I fear a lengthy and at times awkward transition as both the wolves and the land settle into each other. But it is a transition I am eager to observe. It does not feel right to have the wolves locked up in their iron cages, separated from the land, and it does not feel right to have the land void of soil, void of buffalo, overstocked with cattle and void of grass, void of fire, void of wolves. Things do not feel right or natural as they are and often I feel the sense, as when walking in darkness, that we are about to walk into a wall, or step over the edge of some precipice.

It is only partly for the wolves that I want to see them turned loose again. The other part of it is for myself, and my love of this country that I was born into. It matters to me immensely, when I look out at a desert or a mountain range, to know what kinds of animals might still be living there. I don't have to see them. I need only to know that there is the certainty of them somewhere out there—hence the possibility of seeing them, or their sign—and to know also that the land is healthy enough, wild enough, to support them and their secret lives.

The
Land

The graph of sightings and rumors of Mexican wolves still living in the wild is interesting. It rises with steepness rather than with the shallowness you might expect were the increase in rumors due solely to more public education about the rediscovery of a rare species. That awareness may provide some of the fuel for the graph's steep climb—but there appears to be some truth underlying the steepness. In other regions that have graphed a similarly steep increase in sightings of endangered species, the local people really were seeing the animals—the Colorado grizzlies, the recolonizing Montana wolves—before the scientists confirmed or rediscovered them.

Still, there's a mushiness to these rumors, these graphs, too: an irregularity, a question of timing. Wild things come and go in the night, in the rain, leaving no tracks; they cross on stones, they prefer and frequent places not used by humans. Do the increases in rumors reflect that the wolves are already there, or do the increases in rumor compress to a point of saturation, a density of desire in the air, that is finally sufficient to lure and welcome wolves back into that land, as a weather system rolls from a high-pressure area into a low, or as the tides follow the moon around the earth?

There were three sites, three expanses of land, being considered for reintroduction of the captive stock of Mexican wolves: the White Sands Missile Range, near Alamogordo, New Mexico; the Big Bend National Park region, in West Texas; and the Blue Mountains of eastern Arizona, which stretch over into western New Mexico down near the Mexican border.

Wolf activists, particularly in the Southwest, have been working for a solid twenty years to return the lobos to each of these three places. Needless to say it's a hot political issue, especially at the state level—not due just to the livestock industry's fears, but also to worries that big-game hunting revenues will be reduced.

The three sites were studied long if not hard. Often, as biological scrutiny increased, political scrutiny would step in and sidetrack it. The process, the federal law ordering the return of Mexican wolves to their habitat, calls for an Environmental Impact Statement, in which the public's comments must be considered, but among the biologists I spoke with, the Blue Range seems to be clearly the best biological, rather than political, choice.

The other two areas, White Sands and Texas, had some good things going for them as far as wolf-suitable land goes—namely, a sparse human presence—but they also had some fairly dramatic drawbacks. For a while, several years ago, the White Sands range seemed to have the lead, though there were rumors among wolf activists that this location was off limits because the missile range's commanding officer at the time liked to hunt desert bighorn sheep, and was afraid the wolves would eat the sheep.

Some people argue that wolves never lived in the White Sands, only passed through—it's damn dry—while others say that wolves did used to live there. In any event, the things that made White Sands attractive politically were not especially attractive from other perspectives. White Sands is where a lot of "problem" black bears get dumped, to keep them out of harm's way. There are nonnative species, too—African oryx, black as sable, seven feet tall—and, of course, the unexploded ordnance lying here and there, the screaming jet overflights, the echoes of missile detonations, and those shifting, glimmering waves of sand creeping across the landscape, seeming like mirages but very real. . . . White Sands seems only a tad better than the St. Louis or Tucson Zoo, though in the future, who can say? Perhaps this Mad Max vision of nature will be someday ideally suited to a generation or subspecies of "punk" wolves, reared in cities and then, farther into the future, laboratories.

The Texas Solution, as I think of it, was a card that was never even close to being played—not by the hands of humans, at least, or not anytime soon. It seems that if wolves are to return to Texas, they will have to do it on their own. The Texas legislature is even more opposed to wolf reintroduction than is New Mexico, and the Texas livestock industry is even more powerful. The state—my home state—is really dropping the ball on this one, it would seem, though who can say for sure? Does anyone who loves Big Bend National Park's spartan austerity and its lonely, blood-red landscapes want to see millions of tourists funneling down out of Yellowstone to listen to the serenades of Big Bend wolves?

But what really intrigues me about the Texans' meekness is the seeming loss of imagination from that once-free-wheeling culture of imagination and extravagance. There are probably hundreds of Texas ranchers or, rather, landowners—retired oil men—who own giant blocks of land, often for hunting or vacation purposes, literally dirt-cheap lands bought in chunks of fifty and a hundred thousand acres and larger—entire *ecosystems*. Even one of these ranches could provide a core recovery for a few of the wolves; a consortium of three or four neighbors could corner damn near a million acres, home to the only wild Mexican lobos in the U.S. of A. We're talking an entrepreneur's dream: movies, foundation grants, concessions—the right to sell petrified wolf shit through the mail to the yuppie wolf-lovers. . . .

No. The Blue Range called out most clearly, most insistently, for the return of wolves. A committee of USF&WS personnel, in conjunction with wolf biology experts, reviewed the Environmental Impact Statement and settled on the Blue Range of eastern Arizona, in the Apache National Forest, as the best chance the wolves had, from a strictly biological standpoint. Additionally, Arizona's state politics, interestingly, seem to harbor just a shade less resistance to wolf reintroduction—almost like the amount of shadow cast by a fast-passing bird—than the other two states. I think of Arizona's slightly less vehement opposition (powered somewhat by the urban populations of Tucson and Phoenix/Tempe) as being like some zone of weakness or softness, an opportunity to be exploited. I cannot help but think of the phrase *soft underbelly*.

I'm writing about the politics of the regions when what I want to be doing is writing about the land itself, the flora and fauna. But perhaps this is not as unreasonable as it might appear. Certainly the land shapes the politics of a region, being one-half of the equation of time and place that combines to make history —and conversely, on a much tinier scale, politics scratches and furrows at the surface of the land, though it cannot change the land's core, only its surface.

The land. It's big country—the Blue River wolf recovery area, as sketched by the U.S. Fish and Wildlife Service, encompasses 1,032 square miles. The true boundaries of the recovery area will be redefined by the wolves themselves as they begin to have some input into the story—as they begin to redefine their freedom—but for now, not knowing the language or culture of

Mexican wolves, this is the crude and earnest beginning of the story, as told by the scientists to the surface of the land: *Here lies 1,032 square miles into which wolves are to be released, to begin their dialogue with the land, and with us.* (Actually the agency's directive states it a little differently, but that's what they mean.)

The wolves will stray, of course. They will tell, will write with their travels, new stories within that 1,032 miles; and they will spill over and across the edges and boundaries, too. They will dig dens, will scratch at the dirt and uncover old stories, as well, wolf stories, and will retell them, in ways that will replicate or parallel the old stories and movements, with only subtle twists and variations.

The Blue Range country contains an incredible diversity of life forms and, due in part to the harshness of the environment—the heat and aridity—these life forms often contain a uniqueness, a specificity, an *inventiveness*, that seems to pass easily over into the realm we call magic.

It's a feeling you can sense immediately—the kind of sensation we don't like to comment upon, thinking it's something within us, something that others might not feel. But I believe that in places like the Blue Range country or northwestern Montana's Yaak—places of extremes—the source of the sensation comes not from within, but from the land itself, and there is no other or better term for it than *magic*. For this there will never be a unit of measure. You can only feel it, absorb it, then hold it or reject it.

And the Blue has it in spades. There are numerous species of oaks here, for instance. Jerry Scoville, one of the Round River instructors, tells me that the biologist E. O. Wilson pointed out that oaks hybridize readily. The place creates the species, but then the species—the oak—doesn't hold to its constructs, instead doing all manners of morphologically funky, inexplicable, unnameable, and ever immeasurable things: developing and evolving and hybridizing so rapidly that it can't ever be pinned down taxonomically into some sort of classification system. Some struggle is going on with the oaks in southern Arizona, something evolutionarily historic. Something magic. Life *writhing*, shouting to go on. And you can feel it, the incredible density of the richness—the earnest need of the oaks to wrestle a fit, specific relationship with this place and time in which they now find themselves.

   Life.

   Where will the wolves go? The biologists would be foolish to bet, but they must make guesses and attempts to predict this: they must participate, rather than turn away. Almost surely, some wolves will remain secluded in the wilder cores of the Blue Range. And almost surely, too, others will venture out of the recovery area, following perhaps the riparian areas (around which the elk and cattle congregate)—following these seams of moisture that lace the hot dry country like fingers braiding and weaving to bring strength to the land wherever they pass.

   The land leaps in all directions. It climbs from four thousand feet and true desert—sedimentary conglomerates eroding into brilliantly colored canyon labyrinths punctuated with the ancient volcanic leavings of ash, basalt, and obsidian—piñons, oaks, junipers, grasses, cacti, and, along the rivers, cottonwoods, walnuts, ash, box elders—up to nine thousand feet; cool spruce-fir-aspen forests, and the Ponderosa pine forests in the country to the north known as the Mogollon Rim.

The Round River students' 1995 field report described it well:

> "The climate of this area is marked by the same extremes as the vegetation. The average temperature over the area is 47.3° F with temperature ranging from 100° to −32° F. Precipitation is highly varied. The annual average is 20.78 inches with most of the precipitation falling between the months of September and January with extremes of 6.63 and 36.9 inches recorded. At times, the precipitation is concentrated to such a degree that it creates flash floods.
>
> "The land is 99 percent public. There are no permanent residents along the river where the students are working. The nearest communities are Clifton to the south and Alpine to the north.
>
> "The populations of those communities are mainly sustained by mining, logging and ranching. The town of Alpine (population 600), as well as the small ranching communities of Blue and Eagle Creek (about one dozen families), give the primary reintroduction area a low human density of 1.1 people per square mile."

U.S. Fish and Wildlife estimates show that there is also a density of about 1.1 coyote per square mile: one coyote per human.

Where will the wolves go? It is as good a guess as any that they will travel where they have always traveled—the canyons and corridors that are marked anecdotally in trappers' records and old journals from the regions. So much of modern biology tries to force species—especially the larger, less compromising ones—into square holes and pegs where they have never before

existed or flourished: trying to define for those animals, via computers, where their habitat is, rather than letting the grace and fit
of nature, and the irregular polishing of history—the presence of
the animals themselves—dictate what is habitat and what is not.

Again the writings of Brown have much to tell about the
last days of "troubled" wolves. These were usually wolves that had
been crippled—but not caught by a trap—and subsequently often
seemed to turn exclusively to livestock; and whether they did
so for revenge, or because livestock was easier for the wolves to
catch in their crippled condition, only the wolves knew. The wolf
known as Old One Toe, however, was a stock killer even before
he was trapped, as described by Everett Mercer, Arizona District
Agent in charge of predator control in the late 1930s:

> "There was one lobo down along the border near Ruby
> [Arizona], that would invariably rip out the flank of a big
> calf, steer or yearling. Just enough that the bowels came out.
> He always attacked the same way from the rear and flank,
> feeding, just a few bites of flank at a time, while following
> the cripple for a day or so until it died. Then it would cut out
> another fat calf and repeat the performance. It never varied."

After losing all the toes on a foot save for one, Old One
Toe always left his mark by the traps set for him, with that singular toe drawing a line "like the single scratch of a ten-penny
nail, literally pointing directly at each trap set for him," wrote
Brown. It took many years before a government trapper was
finally able to catch up with an aging One Toe.

Other "renegades"—cripples—eluded their trappers for
years before finally being caught in an enfeebled condition. The

Prude Wolf, in Arizona's Galiuro Mountains, was so named because one night in the 1950s it looked in the window at Mrs. Prude. When the Prude Wolf was finally trapped, it was already suffering from a gunshot wound that had been inflicted by a motorist some time earlier.

In Texas, the White Lobo was chased for years but was not killed until 1925, by which time she could neither smell nor hear. She was snow white, except for her gray-tipped tail that, due to her age, was "stiff as a board," reported her killer, Montie Wallace.

Another wolf (also whitish in color), Old Aguila—the most famous wolf in Arizona—ranged in regions of semidesert elevation between 1916 and 1924, "far lower than usual for a wolf," Brown wrote; Old Aguila was "credited with killing many thousands of dollars worth of cattle and sheep . . . One night she reportedly killed sixty-five sheep, and forty another night." According to Gish (1978), she "had a retinue like the tail of a comet, consisting of a large satellite band of coyotes that got fat on 'Old Aguila's' leavings."

(The historian T. H. Fehrenbach reported that in New Mexico in the 1860s, Kit Carson's right-hand man, the Indian-killer Colonel Pfeiffer, attracted a similar retinue: "a legend in his own time, not only among shocked whites, but among the Amerindians, who said that whenever he rode out, the wolves came down from the mountains and hovered behind his column, certain of Indian carrion.")

Another place the wolves will almost surely go is onto the Indian reservation lands—the San Carlos Apache and White Mountain Apache Reservations, cumulatively almost three and a half million acres of prime and historic wolf habitat. The last known lobo in Arizona was killed on the White Mountain Apache land, and reports and rumors of sightings—all unconfirmed—continue to come from the area. Elk herds are "dense," according to a government report. Also found on the reservation are mule deer, antelope, Coues' whitetails, black bears, desert and Rocky Mountain bighorns, and badgers, as are feral dogs; coyotes and mountain lions are common. Hunting permits are sold to non–tribal members.

Whether or not the tribal councils are looking forward to the return of lobos is a matter of conjecture. There are plans by the White Mountain tribe to expand their timber industry into one with value-added capabilities, and to develop a walk-through historical park as a means of broadening a tourist base, but the councils have also adopted resolutions to oppose Mexican wolf recovery in the area—not just on Indian lands, but also on surrounding federal lands—knowing that the wolves, scenting and sighting, *sensing* those pathways from the first half of the century, will fall right back into the old grooves cut for them by their predecessors, passageways whose faint traces may still be visible even on the surface.

Not only do the councils oppose recovery of the Mexican wolf in their area, but they have also adopted a resolution prohibiting U.S. government agencies from gaining access to any wolves—should the wolves return—that venture onto their land.

It's quite an image to picture two of the nation's most vibrant stereotypes—the ragged, antifederalist cowboys and the noble Indians—joining forces to repel the desires of another vibrant stereotype, the wide-eyed urban environmentalists who are trying to push wolves back onto the land.

It's hard to get a good read on the tribal objections—whether they fear increasing livestock depredations, or big-game depredations, or if they just simply don't like being told what to do. It's another wrinkle on this land's surface that will be felt as soon as the wolves hit the ground. Some interpretations of the law say that the wolves, an endangered species, will still belong to the federal government, when they cross over those lines, and other interpretations will say that they belong to the tribes.

Another interpretation is that the wolves belong to neither—that they belong to the deer and elk, that they can be owned no more than a shadow, that they have suffered and endured, lingering near extinction, nearly becoming ghosts, only to squeeze through the iron bars of their captivity just in time—and that it is the land that owns them.

There might be arguments that the environmentalists care more about the wolves than about the Indians, who face traditionally high unemployment; and that the environmentalists certainly care more about the wolves than about the cowboys. Many of the environmentalists will probably wheel (as if turning to protect their flanks) to address these criticisms, allowing a kind of sweet and human wavering, a hesitancy, to enter them, as they become diverted from the initial impulse of justice—of simple right and wrong—and begin instead considering the intricacies of assigning different priorities to different species, different cultures, different religions, different individuals.

The wolves face a tough task here. They are in a bad position, behind bars these last twenty-plus years, and may not be gaining much advantage upon being released. But the land that once owned them is waiting for them and there are still fingers and seams of health and diversity and even magic laced here and there; it is such a big piece of landscape. There is a chance they will make it—and it will be very interesting to see what the landscape yields this next time around, when hope and freedom are entered into the equation.

As was the case with the reintroduction of wolves to Yellowstone and Idaho, a fund will be set up by the private organization Defenders of Wildlife to compensate ranchers for any livestock that is proved to have been lost to wolf predation—even if the losses occurred on public lands.

"We cannot restore wildlife unless we look out for the needs of people too," said the National Wildlife Federation's president, Mark Van Putten. Defenders of Wildlife's Arizona representative, Craig Miller, says, "The only legitimate concern about the Mexican wolf's return is that wolves occasionally do kill livestock. Defenders of Wildlife has stepped in and put our money where our mouth is. We have taken that concern and that potential burden off the backs of the ranchers." (Based on studies in other areas, Defenders estimates that only one-fifth of 1 percent of livestock in the region might be preyed upon by wolves.)

Even if these released wolves disappear, never being seen or heard from again, it seems better than continuing to house them behind bars on into the next century, and if nothing else they will deepen and enrich the mystery of this beautiful red land, causing us to pay more attention to it and to tomorrow, and less to ourselves.

I think they will be indicators—canaries in the coal mine. Their survival, or demise, upon release, will tell us just how far run down the land—and perhaps the immeasurable things associated with land, such as a country's spirit—really is: whether there is anything left on the surface, or whether it's all been used up and washed away, made brittle and numb and sterile.

I am a little nervous about, and a little frightened of, the answer.

THE NEW RANCHER

An interesting thing is happening the longer the Round River students hang out down in this country, spending time in the backcountry and then coming in to attend the town meetings. A lot of the ranchers are getting to know them, and are starting to like them, and are listening to them. Some of the students are even vegetarians, or rather non–beef eaters, and the ranchers are often for the first time seeing the face of the future—yet one more thing that is against them. They're also seeing the young faces of the students themselves and understanding, Hell, she could be my granddaughter, or, Damn, that boy could be my grandson.

As a result, Jerry Scoville, the students' teacher and leader, has a full daybook and is forever juggling his calendar to accommodate the ranchers' requests to have the students over for dinner, and to stay over and participate, if they wish, in ranch activities. For a long time the media (as well as the ranchers themselves) have been speaking of "the death of the cowboy," but I do not believe such a thing can ever happen—not in this country, and especially not in the West—any more than I believe that wolves can be kept out of this landscape.

There are going to be changes and transitions. The land was eroded first, and now, as if in a hundred-year lag or echo, the communities that are based upon that eroded land are under stress, leaning and tilting, sinking; but I do not think the ranchers will disappear. The ranchers, and the rural communities of man, have their own stories and myths within these villages—stories laid across the land like stone walls, connecting those communities to places and events, and to each other. And because they love what they do, those ranchers who desire badly enough to remain ranchers on the public lands will struggle and alter themselves to fit, and refit, that changing land. I believe they will make the adjustments.

It is to Will and Jan Holder's ranch that we have been invited, this spring evening—Jerry, Dennis Sizemore, head of

Round River Conservation Studies, myself, and a visiting high school student and friend of my family, Stephanie, who is a staunch vegan. (Jerry and Dennis and I are delighted, because this means there will be more meat for us.)

The Holders seem young for this business—they're in their late thirties. Their operation—producing what they call "predator-friendly beef"—is so revolutionary that it seems moderate, like so many successful revolutions: it seems now like the only logical, ordered response to a situation.

The Holders don't trap or kill the predators that visit their ranch searching for calves or ailing older cattle. They use herding dogs to keep their cattle moving from pasture to pasture, but that's it as far as protection goes; beyond this, they absorb the losses—on some ranches, these losses can run as much as 10 percent—and then make up for it in the marketplace by as much as 100 percent.

The reason they can do this is that there is a market, a constituency that is affluent and/or willing to pay according to their conscience, and to whom it is worth an extra dollar or two per pound to know that the sirloins they're grilling came from grasslands managed responsibly, and that in eating that steak they are not complicit (beyond the usual complicity of being a taxpaying citizen) in the destruction of predators and fragile rangelands.

It's two hours from the students' camp in the Blues to the Holders' ranch, and we ride through the red-dust beauty of another drought year into the haze of the setting sun. The Holders are standing out in front of their ranch house to greet us when we arrive—we're driving up the long dusty lane, across the barren cobble creek bed of the irrigation ditch and past the windbreaks of big cottonwoods planted by Holder's grandparents years ago.

It's an archetypal scene of America—the old log farm-house squared up and true, the border collie racing alongside our truck, and a few chickens free-ranging here and there, taking dust baths as the sun (behind us now) slips beneath the prairie. Jerry has brought his beautiful yearling springer spaniel with him, Travis, who up to this point has not shown much evidence of caring about birds one way or the other, but upon our arrival we—the ambassadors of wolf recovery and all manners of en-vironmentalism, seeking to calm the fears of the natives—are horrified when Travis leaps out of the truck and makes straight for the henhouse.

There is some squawking and flying of feathers, and then tiny Travis emerges carrying proudly one angry black-and-white hen, fetching it to Jerry.

You're always supposed to reward a bird dog for a good retrieve, so even though the Holders are right there, Jerry takes the hen from his dog's jaws, pats Travis on the head, and says, "Good boy."

The Holders are great. It's not like they haven't seen it—life and death—before. And this hen will live. It's just a little too weird—the friendliness of their operation toward predators.

They invite us in. The farmhouse is gorgeous, with dark old furniture, and the thick time-warped glass of the window-panes takes the last of the day's light and casts it, converts it, into the soft gold rays and slants that I think of as "farm light."

We are handed glasses of wine and head out onto the front porch—passing through the den, which is groaning with books and, seeming conspicuous to me, a fax machine—and we settle into old wicker chairs and hammocks. The Holders are in the midst of a bit of a crisis—their water pump is down, and because of the drought their neighbor has dammed Eagle Creek upstream of them, so that they are essentially without water—but tomorrow will be another day, and they'll resume work on the pump at daylight. In the meantime, there are guests to entertain.

Their decision to return to Will's grandfather's ranch seems to have been one of attrition, of burnout: almost as if they were dying and had to return to this place—or rather come to it for the first time—for medicine. Will was a journalist intern and Jan was a highly successful ad-writing executive for America West airlines. They were working long hours and piling up big bucks and loathing the work and the hot glimmering entrapment of the city—Phoenix—more and more each day.

They broke and ran. Started over. It, like cowboying, is one of the old stories of the West, a story almost as old as fire and the regenerative effects of fire. Perhaps there is something in the soil, and in the western landscape, to authenticate that old myth of the West being the best place for starting over. Whatever the reason—for whatever vaporous yearnings—the Holders started over: one more couple among hundreds of thousands, perhaps obeying some mandate not consciously known by them, only felt.

They were intrigued with Allan Savory's theory, first written about in 1983, of Holistic Range Management (HRM). Like so many powerful or revolutionary ideas, it embraces or at least moves for a while in tandem with that which was previously the enemy. Very basically, HRM—which has since splintered into several subtheories—seeks to reestablish grazing patterns more similar to those with which the landscape and its grazers evolved, before the domestication of those grazers.

For instance, vast numbers of grazing animals have historically moved across the desert or arid grasslands of the world, but the key is that they kept moving, under pressure from predators and also simply to keep grazing new green-growing nutritious grasses, rather than standing around in one spot. The necessity of fire upon the landscape is addressed in HRM. The range historically had rest periods. Basically, the main tenet of HRM is to keep the animals moving around.

This means—unless you're a huge ranch or have formed a co-op—you need lots of gates and fences.

There's a danger, of course, to the power of the theory: both sides can take fundamental aspects of it and focus solely on those parts that suit them. You see or hear of some ranchers saying that high-intensity grazing can duplicate a range fire—just as in the Northwest the timber industry has long been pretending that a clearcut can duplicate a forest fire. Both of these spin moves have just enough of a grain of truth to fool some of the people some of the time.

There is no substitute for fire, just as there is no substitute for air or soil or water. You get the sense, talking to the Holders, that in their personal lives they are in the midst of an extremely metamorphic process—*heat and pressure*—of being refitted to the landscape, and that in their small way they too are engaging with, scratching at, the landscape's surface, so that the new fit—if it is achieved—will not be all one sided, but symbiotic and attached: supple, curved, sculpted, adaptable.

They're viewed as odd birds by their neighbors. There was a bit of a rift last year when one of the neighboring ranchers saw a lion going across their pasture and shot it. He thought the

Holders would be all pleased that he'd done this—never dreamed they'd be *upset*—and the contrariness of the Holders' response seems to have bothered some of the more traditional ranchers more than the presence of the lion itself.

"They couldn't understand it, much less accept it, until we explained to them that it was worth more money to our operation to *not* kill the lions," Will Holder says. "And once we started talking economics, they could get it. But otherwise, they just wouldn't listen. It was like they had this mental block, and the only way they could understand it was through money. It was sad."

Will Holder speaks frankly about their philosophy of ranching. The ranch has sucked up their Phoenix nest egg, and like almost all of the ranches around it—like every ranch, perhaps, that ever was—is in that precarious, eternal tilt between breaking even and failure. But still the Holders' resolve is firm.

Will Holder lists the writings of Wallace Stegner, Wendell Berry, and William Kittredge as having had a major influence on his beliefs. We discuss the Gary Snyder poem "Hay for the Horses"—a favorite of both of ours. The Holders are startlingly clear and straightforward in their understanding that the public lands they lease for grazing do not belong to them. "What right do I have to be here?" Holder asks, speaking of the grazing of his cattle on the public lands. "I have to be receptive to the desires of the public." And with his HRM predator-friendly management, he says, "I am doing what the public wants done with the public land."

"We're not perfect," he adds. "It's impossible to do it perfectly." But they're trying. It appears also that the Holders have a tension to them, discussing their attempts: that there is a high emotional cost of trying to do things right, if not perfectly, rather than just dumping their cattle onto the public leases the same as everyone else, and letting the cattle glean the last of what they can get from these impoverished lands. Perhaps it's "just" the current water crisis, but there is to me the feel of an exhaustion in their plight, as if they are single-handedly attempting to carry too much weight on their shoulders.

It's admirable. The change has to start somewhere.

Driving in, Dennis and Jerry had pointed out the fence lines separating the Holders' leases from various others. There didn't seem to be much of a difference between their rangelands and their neighbors'—in fact, to me the ranges were indistinguishable from each other. The Holders are the first to admit, ruefully, that they haven't seen a difference yet. It's been three years, and it may be ten more before the difference can even begin to be noticed.

It took a long time to get worn down to near-nothing, they explain. "It'll take a little while to come back. It's a long-term commitment."

Perhaps the slight frazzlement, that touch of edginess—call it extreme caution—comes from the stretched-thin passion of the activist. It seems that this dream, this goal—restoring their range to health—is burning them as the prairie fires once consumed the grasslands, cleansing them of clutter and releasing new nutrients with each burn. The Holders are forever writing letters and attending meetings, in addition to their ranch work. Once it's up and running, Holder says, HRM is about 94 percent riding fences, checking to be sure the cattle are in the right allotment, and keeping them moving. Again I think, it's like a pen moving across paper, writing a story—a new one—or rather retelling an old one, even if in miniature at first.

The smell of a roast cooking drifts out to the porch. Some of the dogs have come in from the fields and are gathering at our feet. The wine bottles are emptying into us, as if draining back into the soil. "Niche marketing," is what the Holders are attempting. Under the old system of public-land grazing—or any other kind—they got paid by the auctioneer the same amount, regardless of how they raised their beef. It was just tonnage—volume. But the Holders' meat tastes better, they're certain, and fulfills societal needs. The Holders send out brochures about their ranch to purchasers of their meat. They're aware of the culturewide feeling of a loss of connection and control; they're aware of the physical, even if yet unannounced, need people have to regain some contact with cycles of logic and predictability: the almost physical need, it seems, to participate in the gathering of their food. We want to know where our food comes from, and how it is raised, if we are not doing the harvesting ourselves. Often customers will drive out to visit the Holders' ranch, and will say, with shocked and simple pleasure upon seeing the Holders, "Oh, you're the people in the brochure."

The Holders may call it "niche" marketing, but it's more like gap marketing; it's big enough to drive a truck through. It's strange to consider that the ancient and necessary act of hunting and gathering—picking your own strawberries, milking your own cow, touching your own fields—should be so rare now as to have tangible, quantifiable value.

The Holders are aware they may not make it—the cost of all those fences is eating them alive, as is the price volatility of non-niche beef—and they're trying to diversify. They are experimenting with a winery, and are tossing around some other ideas. They don't want to go back to Phoenix. A certain and true kind of terror seems to arise in their eyes whenever this possibility is mentioned.

"We think we want the same things you want," Will Holder says. "We all want grass-lined creeks with trout in them, and birds, lots of birds, for bird watching."

In an irrigation ditch upstream, where there's still water, is a great blue heron rookery. And in the last bluing of twilight, with violet night drawing across the prairie, we watch bats swoop and dart as if directed not by reason or logic but sheer chance. We watch the long chain of herons returning eastward to their roosting spot, dozens of the long, elegant birds moving slowly across the sky. The wind chimes on the front porch stir, and we search for, and find, one more bottle of wine.

Will Holder answers more of our questions, as he must have answered them a thousand times before for other unbelievers. It could be the late 1800s, and the time of the Wobblies, or the 1920s union fights, or the 1950s. It could be the hippie '60s (have they really been gone for over thirty years?). All of it plays over, again and again, in varying cycles of the same stories, the same responses to the world, and Holder is speaking excitedly now, almost preaching.

"Three meatpacking companies control 80 percent to 90 percent of the nation's beef," he says. "There are a minimum of eight people between our beef and the customer: the driver who takes the cattle to the stockyard, to the auction, to another stockyard, to the slaughterhouse, to the meatpacker, the processor, to the wholesaler, to the retailer. . . . So much fossil fuel is used. We could sell our product quite well overseas—to Japan, for instance—but think of all the calories of fossil fuel it would take to get it there. We'd undo the very thing we're trying to achieve."

The lines of movement—the availability of the niche—are so tantalizing. Instead of going through eight middlemen, how tempting, how powerful, to go straight to the consumer.

"As the system stands now," Holder says, "someone tells me the price I have to receive for my product. I have no option." He's agitated. "Unless I want to change the system. Well, yes, I do want to change the system, and I have the power to do it."

So much is conspiring against him. The laws, as now written, prevent a small operation such as his from crossing state lines. (I think, strangely, of the wolves, when they return, crossing back and forth across borders in the Blue, from Arizona to New Mexico, and across the Indian lands.) NAFTA is not helping matters in the short term, as Mexican cattle, also overstocked on the ranges down there, flood the U.S. market like a dam breaking; nor is the decline in demand for beef helping the Holders' experiment, nor is the near-monopoly of packing houses, nor are the government subsidies of grain. . . .

It occurs to me that this is only another example of what I have always believed: if the land is sick, nothing on top of it can be truly vital or healthy. I fear once again that the wolves may have a tough time of it, and that the Holders will, too.

Jan Holder tells us that it's time for dinner. She's been ducking in and out all evening—before her days as an ad executive, she was a gourmet chef—and tonight's dinner is sinfully spartan: medium-rare roast and baked potatoes from the garden on clean white plates.

It is delicious.

She has saved her firepower, her extravagance, for dessert. It's some flaming thing. There's no telling what all's in it. The outrageousness of it balances the meat-and-potatoes simplicity perfectly: sun and moon. We feel stronger afterward: fortified.

Stephanie—the visiting student—is not eating much. She's at that vulnerable and wonderful age where idealism seems to crest in some wavering triumph before it often begins its long slow deterioration through the rest of one's days, like a mountain crumbling. She's sitting there with martyred poise, surrounded by all these bloody plates and candles, her smile a bit tight; and that's all fine with me, I want her to become who she will become, and I'm proud that I haven't said anything to her about not hurting the Holders' feelings. She needs some room and space to grow—a lot of it. All wildness requires this.

But as she grows quieter and quieter—or rather, as the volume of her silence deepens—it seems that I can read her mind, and I'm a little worried that she's going to mistake the Holders for The Enemy, and begin ranting or chanting the numbers, chapter-and-verse, of the antibeef, antimeat, antifun brigades.

The fact that grazing on public lands produces only 3 percent of this country's beef. The fact that a federal grazing lease costs only about one-fifth of its fair market value, causing, in effect, an annual loss of at least fifty million dollars to the U.S. treasury—a loss that does not even take into account the environmental costs of overgrazing.

The fact that grazing utilizes roughly 75 percent of western public lands.

The fact that there are only thirty thousand permittees in the whole system, controlling these lands.

The fact that. . . .

The wind chimes continue to tinkle. Jan Holder serves us black coffee. I look at our near-empty water glasses—the candlelight trapped within them—and have the awful, irrational worry that I'm looking at the last water on the ranch.

After some more visiting, we say our good-byes, and thank-yous. We ride home in silence, tired—the hour is late—with chicken feathers swirling in the truck and Travis asleep with his head in Jerry's lap. We drive with the windows open. There is a full moon and it lights the desert with a silvery fire. The country down here feels empty without wolves, like the echo of something.

Are we expecting too much to ask them to survive in a land where even the cattle can no longer be sustained?

We have to believe in their ability to find the hidden corners and seams of health, out on the land. We have to believe in their ability to help draw things back together, somehow. But still and again, it seems like an awful lot to be putting on their shoulders.

THE
FEDS

First there's the law, which says plain and simple that the Mexican wolf is an endangered species and must be recovered, if possible: the attempt must be made.

Beneath and below that law, however, lie all the various invisible realities of our culture: the substructure of politics.

Never mind the law, nor the fact that 79 percent of New Mexico residents support wolf reintroduction, as do 61 percent of Arizona residents. Certain moneyed interests have contributed heavily to certain governors and senators and representatives, so that the law has been bent to call the wolves "nonessential" and "experimental," which in theory is supposed to make the 15 percent, or 20 percent, or 34 percent of people who oppose them, depending on where you're doing the polling, not hate the wolves, or the idea of wolves, quite so much.

It's an amazing aspect of our democracy: how the money of so few can purchase such sweeping power—and how the furious passions of so few can similarly influence the law based solely upon the power of their anger or fear or, in some instances, hatred.

These minorities cannot prevent the law—the constructed law—of man, nor the more ordered, flowing laws of nature, from occurring and proceeding. They can only forestall, and momentarily divert, these laws.

The feds get sued by the environmentalists for breaking the law of the land when they cut too much timber or graze too many cattle or withhold the wolves from recovery; but they get sued also by the timber companies and ranchers for breaking the law of money—this afternoon's money—when they don't cut enough timber or graze enough cattle, or when they attempt to recover the wolves. As such, the feds are always between a rock and a hard spot, and you can see their nerves fraying, their tempers thinning: the siege mentality setting in, so that they—BLM and U.S. Forest Service officials—fragment, for self-preservation's sake, and become quasi-military, with their shared

uniforms and the feeling of being under constant barrage. And
you can understand their frustration: their true employers are the
hearts and minds of the American people—the democratic
majority—while the reality is that the ones who do the hiring
and firing—their artificial employers—are the moneyed interests
of the corporate minorities.

The disparity between these two forces conspires to shred
agency officials into further fragments, until they forget how to
act naturally. They are like caged animals, looking back and forth
from one vocal constituent to one moneyed constituent, and
rarely these days do they have time or even authority to look
at the forests, or the range, or the grizzlies, or the wolves themselves—much less the time or authority to look at the future or
the past. Science in our government is becoming extinct, as it
lingers trapped too long between those two savage forces.

It has always been this way, but it seems that more than
ever the situation is becoming untenable.

Dennis and I are at a Mexican food restaurant in
Albuquerque with a couple of Fish and Wildlife Service folks—
Dave Parsons and Wendy Brown, lead coordinator and assistant,
respectively, for the reintroduction project—who have come up
here on a Sunday, their day off, to fill us in on the recovery
process from their perspective, and to answer questions. They've
gone to great lengths to answer, in print, almost every possible
question that could ever be asked about Mexican wolves—chief
among them the unanswerable "Can they adapt from the zoo to
the wild?" Only time can answer that one.

The red wolves that have been introduced from captivity
to the Carolinas are now into their second and third generations

of successful offspring, so it can be done, though anyone who would extrapolate from North Carolina to Arizona must prepare for the unexpected. Dave and Wendy are scientists, but our conversations seem to veer from the very beginning toward politics and, having established that course, seem unable to break out of it. Perhaps it is all my fault: perhaps when they asked me what I wanted to talk about, I should have asked them about paw widths and lengths. I should have asked them about the wild-conditioning pens planned for the Sevilleta National Wildlife Refuge in New Mexico, from which some of the wolves will be selected for release into the wild (electric fencing, chain-link fences, gates buried four feet deep that rise ten feet high with no gap larger than two inches, and so on, and on.)

But politics seems the order of the day: politics and margaritas. In a nutshell:

Texas is out as a reintroduction site because of the strong antiwolf politics.

White Sands has a lot of mountain lions, which might prey on the city-soft wolves, and also has less water than does the Blue Range.

Arizona—the Blue Range—isn't Yellowstone, but it's clearly the best site from a biological standpoint. There's some squabbling going on between the game and fish commissions of Arizona and New Mexico, despite their constituents' support of wolf reintroduction—the Arizona Game and Fish Commission passed a resolution supporting wolf reintroduction in New Mexico, and the New Mexico Game and Fish Commission passed a resolution supporting wolf reintroduction in Arizona.

(Also slightly complicating things from a political perspective, the Blue Range crosses over into New Mexico.)

It reminds me exactly of the recently designated Grand Staircase/Escalante National Monument in southern Utah, 1.8 million acres of public land that the Republican legislature of Utah was trying to grab for the purpose of an immense low-grade coal mine. Never mind that over 70 percent of Utahns, and Americans, wanted the land kept as it was—the Utah Republicans, elected by the big corporations, went after it anyway. President Clinton came in, ignored the Utah senators and representatives, listened directly to the will of the people, and created, or rather preserved, that red desert for America in perpetuity. (And in so doing, I fear, possibly let himself off the hook of criticism for his failure to permanently protect forested public roadless areas in the Northwest—but that is another matter not yet linked to Mexican wolves.)

I mention to Dave and Wendy my fear that the United States is convoluting, is undergoing some horrible metamorphosis wherein the western half of the country—containing the remaining bulk of our natural resources—is fragmenting, being leveraged into some awful, ailing kind of puppet state, like Chechnya or Afghanistan, in which the people's desires are ignored to serve the larger corporate megaliths. I confess that my fear is that the majority of western governors have ridden corporate donations to their current positions of power, outspending their opponents on TV and radio ad time by margins of three to one, five to one, even ten to one; that the western Republican governors are now acting to liquidate anything on public lands that's not nailed down; and that it's the public's duty to future generation, to nail down what we can, and to turn the thieves and plunderers back.

Strong talk, for a Sunday. I get the feeling that even on their off day, it's best if Dave and Wendy don't pursue this discussion. There's a bit of a silence, after which they ask me what it's like in northern Montana: meaning not the politics, but the countryside. *Biology*; we ease back into it.

Except that they do offer this: governors "come and go," and the volatility of such political repositioning makes the feds' job much harder.

I start to comment that all death throes have a certain spasticity to them, but decide I've been dire enough; they need encouragement, not discouragement. I try to think of something biological. But then Dave and Wendy mention politics again— that even though the Draft Environmental Impact Statement was finished in 1995, they suspect it won't be until after the November '96 elections that the Final EIS comes out (this turned out to be the case); and that if wolf supporters are serious about recovery efforts, they'd better get their pens and paper out and send in some letters, because the opponents of wolf reintroduction, though small in number, have been busy at the typewriter.

The air force, for instance, has written, fearful that wolves will interfere with their airspace over the national forests in a manner "not unlike the restrictions the spotted owl has placed."

The army has written, the Apaches have written. The game and fish commissioners have written—all with one form of opposition or another—as have the governors.

Where are the wolf's advocates? The grand total of respondents, on both sides, has been a measly 17,374, including the Arizona Wool Producers Association, the New Mexico Wool Growers, and the Blue River Cowbelles.

Hell, the Lava Soil and Water Conservation District is even against reintroduction, which really chaps my britches. (Wrote the LSWCD, "Let's support the Mexican wolf—in the Albuquerque Zoo, where the wolf enthusiasts can visit him all the time." The feds' laconic, courteous response? "Thank you for your comment.")

Wendy explains that the public opinion polls and surveys are showing us what we already know in our guts—the invisible thing we can feel in the air—that the people who are against reintroduction feel frightened and disconnected and hence insecure and angry.

"They don't hate the wolf specifically," she says. "They just view it as one more example of the loss of control in their lives." You can blame part of this invisible unease on corporate restlessness in the days of monopolies and mergers. Or you can blame it on something more spiritual and pervasive—on a trauma to the soul of the land itself, and our disconnected, semi-electronic relationship to it. In many ways the opponents of wolves seem so much like the wolves themselves that it is wildly ironic: though their numbers are small, they seem to retain a core fierceness that cannot be ignored—nor would you want to, for fear is one of the most primal emotions of any place. It's never going to go entirely away—not in a wild, healthy ecosystem.

Dennis tells us a story about Jerry Scoville and his first night down in the desert. Jerry had driven down from his home outside Seattle—a day and a night on the road—and was whipped. He wasn't going to be able to make it all the way into the Blue that night. He was out on some forever-stretch of prairie, it was dusk, so he pulled over onto the shoulder and leaned his seat back and rubbed his sandy eyes, watched the lurid sunset, and fell deep asleep for the night.

Jerry says he woke shortly after midnight to the cold steel of a revolver stuck in his ear.

"Just what do you think you're doing here?" a voice demanded.

It was no time for smart-aleck answers, such as "Sleeping," or "Visiting Arizona—the Sunshine State," or even "Well, actually at this moment, shitting my britches."

The gist of that shadowy conversation was that the countryman believed that the Washington State license plates on Jerry's car indicated that it was from Washington, D.C.; that the countryman had caught a spy, an infidel from that foreign land, napping within his territory.

Jerry had to show him his driver's license, with the street name and the town—"Seattle, Washington"—to convince him he wasn't a fed.

Jerry says he left out the part about how he was a biology professor working to restore the Mexican wolf to its native habitat. He was allowed to continue on his way. He was allowed to live.

Sure, a lot of it's hype. This really happened, and there's nothing hyperbolic about a pistol stuck in your ear—that's flat-line reality—and yet, in the reporting of it, the press gravitates toward the detailing of these sorts of extremes rather than chronicling the much larger biomass, or story-mass, of the events and emotions in the middle.

And yet these extremes, such as the pistol-waving *paisano*, the Unabomber, or militiamen, do need reporting, in addition to the main story. These extremes have sociologic power beyond symbolism, and power beyond the establishment of a story's physical outer boundaries and parameters.

Again, these stories from the fringes are like the wolves themselves: perhaps there are only ten or twelve of them out there, or a hundred or two hundred, but in their compressed isolation they have achieved, it seems, some kind of core density—a power—a fire of sorts, which will either finally smolder and blink out, or explode, fragmenting that middle ground around it, and in so doing giving birth to new philosophies, new ways of being. . . .

Which, in the manner of geology, will always only seem like a new story to the fresh observer; though they have all already been told from the very beginning. There are no new stories in nature, only new observers.

Even among the thirty thousand ranchers who hold permits to graze cattle on the public lands, 21 percent, or sixty-two hundred of them, support wolf reintroduction.

The mainstream numbers hardly ever get reported: the fact that Catron County, New Mexico, for instance—deep in the shadow of the wolf recovery area and home of the vitriolic "Wise Use" movement, a corporate-sponsored facade of grassroots activism for "states' rights"—is comprised now of almost 50 percent nonnatives, and that most of those immigrants are refugees from the suburbs of California. You won't read either that over 50 percent of the residents in the Catron County area support wolf reintroduction. The only stories that make the wire concerning Catron Country are the ones like Jerry's, or the stories about the

crazy piss-ant local politicians, nutty county commissioners trying to drum up reelection support by shooting at helicopters or
preaching about the Red, or Pink, or Yellow, or Green Menace.
You can find this in Catron County, New Mexico, or Nye
County, Nevada, or Lincoln County, Montana. You can find a
few disillusioned, angry, justifiably bitter individuals—brittle but
momentarily powerful in their isolation—in the last summoning
of their rage. If you're not careful, the momentary power of these
lone or loosely connected responses can fool you into thinking
that this is how things really are. These responses can mask the
greater attributes of a community—the hidden, permanent well-
springs of hope; the willingness to help anyone down on his luck;
the members' great friendliness and loyalty among themselves.
Tenderness, goodness, is as prevalent in these communities as
anywhere else in the country, or more so.

    In Alpine, Arizona, Dennis and I had one small inci-
dent, in the gas station. We were visiting with the store owner,
talking about hunting, and when asked why we were there, we
told him about our hopes for the wolves. We had the usual
conversation, well tempered and respectful but passionate, about
government interference, government regulation, and the
United Nations—"You guys are all right," the owner conceded,
"you'll at least *listen*"—but then something strange happened:
the name *Bruce Babbitt* was mentioned, and the man's demeanor
changed as if thrown by a switch. All reason and, it seemed,
humanity, left him—his face went stiff—and he replied coldly,
barely able to speak, so great was his hatred, that "the only
problem with Bruce Babbitt is that he is alive." And that was
the end of that conversation.

A well-dressed man in a suit and black cowboy hat who'd been standing in the back of the store behind us, listening—he did not appear to have ever done a day's worth of physical labor in his life—picked up an ax, swung it lightly in our direction a few times, nodded to the store owner, and walked out with it, still swinging it like a baseball bat and smiling. "Gonna split some *wood*," he said mysteriously.

And on our way to a camping spot that night—we passed our turn—we realized an old white truck was following us, for when we turned around to go back to our turnoff, it did too, though it didn't follow us down to our campsite and was, I think, only another invisible kind of scent marking, a sort of subtle harassment or wolflike territoriality.

But that was just that one little spike of an incident— that one little burr. We also saw the mainstream of friendliness.

On Dennis's and my swing through Catron County, in our shiny red rented sport-utility vehicle that identified us so clearly as outsiders, it seemed that all the county's residents— none of them knowing who we were or what we were there for, only that we were from the outside—went out of their way to wave to us as they passed on the road: as if consciously trying to represent themselves accurately as friendly, not mean; as if hurt by the image the outside world was forming of them. Ten or twelve trucks in a row went past one morning, each giving that wave across the steering wheel.

Without doubt, the communities are being stretched thin by this century's end, as are the wolves. Environmentalists in the next century are going to have to go both ways instead of just one: will have to be both fiercer and more tolerant—a tough position, but one that the situation demands. We must adapt or fail. We must take care of the wolves and yet concern ourselves, too, with the rest of the system—the increasingly huge society of man, that immense biomass in the middle—without compromising our beliefs and values.

The social stresses of human economic and cultural transition, and economic recoveries, are well documented. The wolves will have their own stresses.

Parvo virus, canine distemper, infectious canine hepatitis, leptospirosis, rabies—all are in greater concentrations now, due to domestic dogs, than they were the last time the Mexican wolves were out and about, free and at large.

Mites, ticks, fleas, heartworm, tapeworm, hookworm; any of a thousand stresses could accumulate upon them, here at century's end, to be one stress too many, and the wolves could disappear, could blink out. They could hybridize with coyotes, rather than killing the coyotes, and disappear in that manner—again, blinking out—for a few millennia.

Or they could find root-cracks of survivability and explode with dramatic success into the next century, the next cycle.

THE FLY IN
THE OINTMENT

It's tempting at this point for either a journalist or a storyteller
to spend some time detailing the decades-long struggles of the
individuals who, in the beginning, were almost the sole supporters of Mexican wolves. It was not that long ago that it—Mexican
wolf recovery—was considered a pipe dream. Twenty and thirty

years ago (it seems like yesterday), it seemed a radical, doomed way to waste your frenzied time. Crusaders such as Bobbie Holaday, who in 1988 founded PAWS—Preserve Arizona's Wolves—began their work as a classic subculture of grunge-mimeograph rantings, near-solitary voices in the desert dreaming of a reality—wolves returning to the Southwest—others thought was impossible. Susan Schock, whose ferocious commitment to the desert and her attempts to defend it against overgrazing led to the formation of Gila Watch. It raises the interesting question of what radical ideas are out there today with regard to the protection of wildness and the environment; what mainstream awaits us in another twenty years.

The Wildlands Project and the Northern Rockies Ecosystem Protection Act (NREPA) are two that come to mind, though as visionary as they are, they are only bittersweet to me in that they are not radical enough. (I'd like them to pay more attention, respectively, to my beloved Yaak Valley at the other end of the world from the Mexican border, where my own attention is now drawn.)

On one hand, most citizens recoil from a certain unthinking, throbbing kind of radicalism—the injustice or unfairness implicit so often in its all-sweepingness, when justice and fairness are the very things most radicals claim to be fighting to defend. But on the other hand, I worry that there is not enough radicalism left; that it is as if the last radical ideas are preserved in history books or behind the iron bars of the past, and that there are none viable out there now on the horizon, nor are any forthcoming for a long time, as a certain sleepiness settles over that which is left of what was once a wild land.

I wonder: are we having radicalism bred out of us? What does it say for us when the idea of having one hundred Mexican wolves free in the world again is deemed radical?

There is a radical living down near Patagonia, Arizona— in what was once Mexican wolf country, and from which reports still issue of sightings of wolves and the sounds of their howls. (I heard such howls myself some miles east of Patagonia, about eight years ago.) Dennis Parker, a self-taught biologist—a consultant—doesn't want the captive wolves released into the wild, and though he's sent hundreds, perhaps even thousands of letters to government agencies over the last couple of decades detailing why, it's still kind of difficult to get a handle on his reasons. Some people dismiss him as being a pro-cattle lackey, or just another antigovernment guy, but what Parker will tell you is that he simply doesn't like seeing things done the wrong way, and that he basically doesn't think the Mexican wolf has a chance in hell. The cliché of *pariah* comes to mind, listening to him criticize the proposed recovery. His anger has a bit of the terror to it that such angers often contain, and yet even though he's on the opposite side of the fence from me—he doesn't want the wolves turned loose; I do—I have a fascination with his passion, and a respect for the fundamental fury and the tens of thousands of hours he has spent for no profit other than what seems the staunching and bulwarking of his idealism. He could just as easily be me, protesting some awful timber sale, some brute government heavy-handedness being manipulated by the corporate puppet strings above.
My interpretation is that Parker's voluminous protests boil down to two key issues: one, he believes that a lack of genetic

variability among the captive wolves dooms the project, and the species, from the start; and two—a corollary—there may still be wild wolves down in Mexico, that should be given every chance to recolonize naturally. This is the way, Parker argues, that speciation and survival and evolution should occur.

He's not going to win this argument. But he's sure as hell not going to give up. And if you can put aside the baseline motivation for his protests—livestock hardliner, or biological purist, or, at some deeper level, simply the fly that must be in every ointment—his complaints and fears and criticisms, whether or not they are proved by history to have been accurate, serve a useful purpose in the current dialogue.

It's interesting to me, listening to Dave Parsons and Wendy Brown discuss their opposing force: the man who's trying to stop them from doing their job. Dave becomes as animated in talking about Parker as he has been in discussing the wolves, which up to this point are after all captive, semidomestic animals, while Parker is wild and free. Soon the wolves will be moving in Parker's direction, like some lines of conflict charted by the heavens—some *fate*—and his predictions, or protests, will be proved true or false; but right now the two sides stand at full tension.

Parker will be either right or wrong, but either way the distance between them will close. There will never be this much space between them again. That the wolves are coming back is a sure thing, a given; the process, as mandated by the people's law, is in electroglide. Just as sure in the world is the utter, almost *quivering* ideological resistance to their return held firmly by Parker.

I want to believe that Parker's resistance does not cloak some grazing agenda; that his is a pure and elemental response to the process he sees unfolding. I want to believe that these kinds of individual responses—this kind of ferocity—still remain in the world, and among us.

Parker responded to the Draft EIS—which made a preliminary recommendation, based on biology, that the Blue Range was the superior release site of the three alternatives—with what the U.S. Fish and Wildlife Service described as "a lengthy, detailed, unpublished paper entitled, '*Reintroduction of the Mexican Wolf: Instrument of Recovery or Instrument of Demise?*'"

In what appears to be an unprecedented response, the USF&WS devoted an entire section of their Final EIS to the Parker Problem, under a chapter called "Response to Parker Comment." (Complete copies of the Parker paper and the responses are available for review at the USF&WS regional office in Albuquerque.)

The end result of the feds' response to Parker's response was kind of like a lopsided basketball game. The USF&WS gathered fifteen of the country's leading experts on genetics, conservation biology, and wolves—a scientific Dream Team of sorts—and proceeded to disintegrate Parker's paper. It was not a pretty sight, and though I side with the views of the scientists (twelve Drs., one Ms., and two Misters)—whose unanimous opinion was that Parker had skewed individual facts and concerns, selecting from them only the fundamental fragments that could then be molded or shaped to substantiate his fears—there still exists (for me) in the firmament of his presentations enough of that lingering doubt, that uneasy insecure feeling, for the whole exchange to be fascinating and, I believe, of sociologic and perhaps even scientific merit. I think it did the scientific community good to be forced to line up together upon being attacked and say, in essence—without the usual scientific hedging of bets—affirmatively and with consensus, *This is why we think the wolves should be turned loose.*

One example of Parker's criticism—his contention, his assertion, that the wolves will not make it—refers to an effort up on Coronation Island, in southeastern Alaska, to release some captive-raised gray wolves there. The wolves did fine for a while, but then, as Parker noted, they died out. Parker referred to this failure as an "extinction."

To a one, the scientists pointed out that the Coronation Island wolves died not because they were unsuccessful at adapting to the wild, but because they were too successful. The island was too small—a closed system—and they exhausted their prey base: they ran out of deer to eat.

The successful red wolf reintroduction in North Carolina and the Great Smokies—which relied upon the release of captive wolves—was cited by several scientists, and Dr. Edward Spevak, of the Wildlife Conservation Society, noted that "the use of captive bred animals for reintroduction has also shown itself to work in a number of cases, e.g. Arabian oryx, golden lion tamarin, American bison, Andean condor, and the red wolf. The argument that because one small isolated wolf introduction eventually failed no further attempts should be made is ludicrous."

The clincher to my way of thinking, however, comes from Norma Ames, the former leader of the Mexican Wolf Recovery Team, who wrote, "The answer to the question of whether reintroduction will 'conserve the Mexican wolf' seems to me to be that we cannot know for sure. We can, however, be fairly sure that keeping Mexican wolves *only* in captivity will not achieve that end."

Moving to the meat of Parker's concerns—and mine, and, I believe, everyone's who is associated with or has an interest in the project—Parker raises the truly troubling matter of the questionable genetic diversity in the captive population. It's all a bit over my head—the respondents, the scientists, are throwing around terms and phrases such as "the retention of 90 percent of initial quantitative genetic variation for 200 years" and "the management of the certified line [of Mexican wolves] has been excellent and professional in all respects and has only resulted in an average inbreeding coefficient of 0.184 for the living animals after nearly twenty years (approximately five generations) of captive breeding. With a small number of founders, this is a very impressive record and is probably as small an increase as could be possible." (Dr. Phil Hedrick, Arizona State University, Mexican Wolf Recovery Team.)

Parker cites various studies that show captive wolves as vulnerable to inbreeding, but does not mention the study done by Dr. David Mech, National Biological Service, who wrote, "In the wild, the Isle Royale [of northern Michigan] study suggests that apparently deleterious gene combinations are selected out, thus cleansing the population and allowing the better combinations to survive and maintain the population."

As evidence of the inbreeding Parker believes is occurring in the captive Mexican wolves he noted that some of the Mexican wolves—as with the Florida panther, which is undeniably suffering from inbreeding due to lack of varied individuals (fewer than fifty remain) in the diminished population—are being born with malformed testicles.

In certain instances, this condition (monorchidism or cryptorchidism) might result in reduced fertility, though it's debatable whether or not it's prevalent enough in the captive wolves to be a problem.

Certainly it's a concern—or the shadow of a concern. But unexamined, or underexamined, it seems, is the stress and desensitizing of captivity versus the tonic of the wild. Dr. Spevak wrote, "The cheetah is a case in point. This species shows less genetic variability than Mexican wolves and survives in large numbers in the wild where there is habitat protection and no human persecution. There is presently nothing to indicate that this would not also be true for the Mexican wolf."

Dr. Philip Miller of the World Conservation Union logged in: "A metric commonly used to assess the severity of inbreeding depression is the number of lethal equivalents contained within the population. An analysis by Ralls et al. (1988) of 40 captive mammal populations revealed that the number of lethal equivalents ranged from 0 to 30, with a median of 3.14. I have performed a similar analysis of inbreeding depression in the current Mexican wolf captive population (Miller and Hedrick 1995) and concluded that, with respect to both survival to 180 days and to individual weight, inbreeding depression is not detectable. The number of lethal equivalents in the pedigree, calculated using a method identical to that used by Ralls et al. (1988), was found to be 0.136. Statistical analysis shows this value to be indistinguishable from zero."

Dr. Rolf Peterson of Michigan Technological University admonished, "I underscore the importance of release in the wild if the current captive stock is to serve a useful purpose; their potential contribution diminishes with each generation."

Give one of the good doctors a beer or two, and perhaps the advice might be even blunter: *Turn the sons of bitches loose and let the land decide.*

The feds' reactions to the rest of the respondents involved in the public comment on the EIS was noticeably subdued: a startling contrast in tone, due probably to the fact that they did not feel as threatened. Their core fears, our core fears, were probably not touched as deeply as they were by Parker's arguments. The feds listened to each and every comment impassively before responding with an almost catechismlike intonation.

The De Baca County (New Mexico) Commissioners wrote: "We do not need wolves in our area in the future nor do the urban areas need these either. If urban area had lived [sic] and been exposed to coyotes, and perhaps wolves, I cannot believe the majority of the people would want the introduction of wolves into the State of New Mexico."

Responded the feds: "Thank you for your comment. Wolf recovery is not proposed for De Baca County."

Jack Brown, of the Arizona House of Representatives, wrote, "I think there are many reasons why this is not a good idea. . . . I think we need to make a better environment for the Mexican wolf in a controlled situation, such as a large area in a zoo that would give them natural habitat but from which they could not escape. I just do not think we need to turn the clock backward."

The Texas Parks and Wildlife Department wrote, "[We request] that the Service take no actions to reintroduce the Mexican wolf to Texas."

The feds' response, again: "Thank you for your comment."

The county commissioners seem to represent the mouth-pieces of old-line minority interests, and in many cases fears, riding luxuriously on a lack of research into the situation. Parker's response, though often scientifically errant, strikes deeper chords. The feds don't agree with him, but I think it's safe to say that he's been represented in the process, and heard.

Perhaps I'm being naive, holding out hope that he truly wants the wolf to survive—for it to recolonize up from Mexico naturally—and that he's not just trying to block the recovery. This naïveté is a habit I have not yet been able to shake.

What I want to believe is that Parker is like some kind of country rock—some clastic, insoluble, unerodable, crooked, jagged thing floating along in the magma of change.

Walking the side canyons of the country in the Blue Range, you'll often see ancient river-washed walls of conglomeratic mudstone—lithified sediments, the dried slurry of ancient floods, filled with cobbles and even boulders that were washed along in the old floods' great energy and deposited among that mud slurry as if stranded, but still unbroken—strange reminders of different times and different lands, refusing to yield, even as they are swept along by a changing landscape.

THE CAPITALIST

S lowly, irresistibly, I find myself being drawn out into that most dangerous, vulnerable, and indefensible of positions, hope. I tell myself once again to stay objective, and to never lose sight of the bottom line, the one-sentence description of this project: our government *is going to take captive, semi-domestic*

*Mexican wolves and turn them out into a landscape vastly reduced in
ecological health.*

But increasingly, as the project proceeds, there is less
room for my cynicism. Fear begins to be crowded out by the sheer
busy-ness of hope; by the swelling wave of it. For every old fart
with worries and concerns, there is a young fart with fire in her
blood, fire in his heart. There always has been. I can find no finer
antidote to despair than youth.

Except that in 1997, it's not all young people. There is
another season of Round River students, and camping here with
them are youthful AmeriCorps workers—but also in their midst
are men and women in their forties and fifties, volunteers, who
have come to help the wolves.

We're camped on one of Ted Turner's big New Mexico
ranches. With over a million acres of land, he's the largest
landowner in the state. It's a dry landscape, sere, with most of its
color locked in the frozen embrace of the rocks—bands of black
and red. Grama grass waves in the wind, and the granitic hills are
dotted sparsely with yucca, sotol, and mesquite and juniper. Oaks,
cottonwoods, and sycamores grow giant and shady along the
creeks. Visible to the west lie the cool blue mountains—New
Mexico's Gila National Forest and Arizona's Blue Range, where
the Mexican wolves will be released next spring.

As the project proceeds, more captive-breeding and
"candidate selection" facilities are needed—more halfway houses
for the captive wolves, as some of them, or their offspring, pass
(we hope) from zoos to halfway houses to soft-release pens and
then, finally, to the wild—and so Turner stepped in. His ranch is
not too far from the Blues—similar country, with similar eleva-

tions—and he offered to house the wolves: to construct more captive breeding facilities. The Turner Endangered Species Fund, supported on this particular project by the Turner Foundation, footed the bill. They hired a contractor, a builder, by the name of Tom Savage—his real name—to oversee the project, and they decided to use volunteer labor to construct the holding pens. A cynic could say they did it for the public relations value and an optimist would say they did it for reasons of democracy, or spirit— and a pragmatist might say they did it for both of these reasons, or somewhere in between. I don't really care, personally. All that stuff is behind the wave, anyway, and already has fallen into dim history and dust. The forward momentum of the wolves, and the space they will occupy once again, is what we are looking at, out in front of us, out in the near future.

No one knows whether any of the released wolves—if any of the captive breeders in Turner's new facilities, or their progeny, are ever selected for the wild—might someday return to the ranch. And perhaps if any wild wolves still remain in Mexico, they will somehow catch the scent and hear the howls of "Turner's wolves," and will venture north to find and breed with these newcomers.

This coming wave or generation of wolves, due in to Turner's ranch later in the winter, arriving from zoos around the country, probably won't ever see freedom—unless, after being released into the halfway houses on his ranch, they exhibit irresistibly wild characteristics. More likely, their pups are the ones who will benefit and be released into the wild in future years; raised here not in a zoo, but in the spartan pens, closer to the mountains and as free from human contact as possible in their growing-up years.

But they're being observed and evaluated all the while—measured, in our mind's eye, against the landscape: as if we are little gods or artists capable of judging such a fit, such a match.

There is no choice for us but to try.

We're camped by a creek beneath giant cottonwoods, listening to their leaf-rattle all night, and to the slow trillings of crickets, the yappings of coyotes, and the gruntings of javelinas. The ranch has set up crisp big tents for the volunteers, so that it looks, I suppose, like some African safari. The volunteers—roughly a dozen—are fed; Tom Savage's wife, Linda, is an amazing cook and spends each day, all day, preparing their meals. In turn the volunteers have only to dig and claw at the ground, preparing a place and a way for the coming of the wolves.

It would be easy to the think of Turner Endangered Species Fund as possessing a Hollywood kind of mentality, as being interested mainly in the glamorous, high-profile species—the wolves, the whales, the manatees—which would, in my opinion, still be wonderful. But the Fund isn't like that. They're working to reestablish black-footed ferrets on the ranch, and California condors, and desert bighorn sheep, it's true, but also endangered species you might never have even heard of: the optima falcon, and rare plants and fishes, and native pollinators like the sphinx moth.

Buffalo are living on the ranch as well. We're on one of the smaller ranches—the three-hundred-thousand-acre Ladder Ranch, which Turner bought five years ago. There were only about three thousand head of cattle run on the ranch at the time he purchased it, and he's replaced the cattle with one thousand buffalo. The ranch was in good ecological health then, and it's only getting better.

There aren't any fences around the ranch's perimeter. The buffalo haven't shown any signs of leaving, however, in these last five years, and I wonder if it's because they can sense or know that things are not so fine to the north and the south and the east and the west, or if there is some more troubling component to their seeming complacency. Have they forgotten, as a culture— have they lost the lesson of the seasonal migrations, the autumnal drifts? Don't the stars, and the spin and pulse of the earth, order these things?

How does nature work? What makes it run? What process, if any, is required to get those buffalo moving again? A stronger wind from the south—a nudge from, or even the sight or odor of, a wolf—a recollected memory, wafting in one day like a dream? Elk bugle in the high mountains of the national forest beyond; the bulls wander onto the ranch at the start of the hunting season, though they are hunted on the ranch, too, for eighty-five hundred dollars an animal. Such ecological bounty protected on private lands while the surrounding public lands suffer, in places, at the hands of extractive industry, begs a discussion of feudal estates, the Jeffersonian Commons, and the very essence of capitalism—supply and demand, resources and labor—but, like most people, I just don't want to fool with it. I just want the wolves to get out of captivity and to have their best shot. I don't think any of us is any purer than anyone else. The capitalist savagery of Pegasus Gold and Anaconda Copper, the bone-crushing indifference and the mindless insatiability of the international timber companies, and the spinelessness of government—these things make me rail, but I've still eaten a french fry or two at McDonald's, I've flown on a jet, ridden in a car, and traded and bartered with the currency of the land. I need wilderness, big wilderness, as an antidote to my sins—a place to say, *Here I will finally devour nothing*—and I really need those wolves to make it, despite the longest of odds. It's not the "ownership" of the land that bothers me, it's the treatment of it. Some public land is managed better than some private land; some private land is managed better than some public land. I don't think the signatory on the deed matters much to the wolves, the cottonwoods, the rivers, or the stars.

Tom Savage wants to do everything by hand. No cement mixers, no bulldozers: just human beings. The five holding pens—the halfway houses, Ted Turner's Halfway House for Troubled Wolves—will be constructed on steep south-facing slopes, to help the wolves get used to the warmth, and to also encourage them to dig dens. At the tops of the steep pens—each about one-third of an acre in size—there is a level area where the wolves will be fed and, if necessary, tended to by a vet. Entire freezers of gutted, roadkilled deer and elk are awaiting the wolves' dining experience; for the last couple of years, an AmeriCorps volunteer, Keith Rutz, has been prowling the Southwest, gathering wild game from the roadside ditches in anticipation of this day. The thawing will soon begin. Frozen elk melting back into meat for the wolves: motionless meat, not meat on the hoof, but a start nonetheless. Blocks of frozen deer melting, and wolves, frozen in captivity for seven generations, finally melting back out onto the landscape.

I know the odds are long: extraordinarily long, it seems to me, some days. But being around the students and volunteers as well as seeing their work on the physical actualities of the release, seeing something you can touch with your hand, a thing of heft, of specific density—the release pens—does wonders for my hope. The project is going forward. The time for too-much-worry is all in the past, and energy poorly spent, at that. The wolves are coming, and being around these volunteers, especially the young people, you get the feeling that they can't be stopped.

There is a carver in our midst. His name is Jay Nochta. He's a big man, looking strong as a draft horse—not a big talker. In fact, for the two days Dennis Sizemore and I are there, we will not hear him volunteer a single word on his own, unsolicited. He's not standoffish or aloof, just quiet.

Straightaway Jerry takes me over to meet Jay and to look at a couple of the carvings Jay's been working on in his spare time—working with just a pocketknife and a piece of Arizona walnut he found on the ranch.

One carving is of a fence swift—Jay's just begun it, but already you can see the perfect form emerging from out of the wood—and the other, a tree frog resting on a leafy branch, is finished, and is so exquisite that it makes my eyes water just to look at it. Every rib and vein in the frog is present, as is every rib and vein in the carved leaves. When Jay hands it to me I cup it in both hands as if it might leap away from me. It is the finest carving I have ever seen.

Jay's pleased with my reaction. When I ask him if he's ever carved a wolf before, he nods and says that he did once. He did it for a fund-raising benefit for Preserve Arizona's Wolves.

"They liked it a lot," he says, but shrugs, indicating he didn't think it was his best work. Bobbie Holaday is the person who put Jay in touch with the Ladder Ranch. Initially Jay was going to work just two weeks, but he liked it so much that he asked to stay on for the whole term—he's been here seven weeks now, with seven more to go—and Tom Savage is thrilled to have him.

"It feels good to be working with my hands," Jay says.

They call it "going up on the hill"—heading across the ridge each morning to the eight hours of grueling manual labor. Dennis and I are a little surprised at first—Dennis had intended to lecture the students on conservation biology, and I had a little talk planned about literature—but Tom Savage gives us each a pair of leather gloves and puts a pickax in our hands with an air of unnegotiability that tells us there is no time now for poems— not unless I want to sing them out while busting through the ghost-white layers of caliche and rolling aside boulders with the pry bar.

Solar panels will provide energy to pump water for the wolves to drink. There are work details strung out all over the mountain, erecting fences, laying water lines, burying tanks: all by hand.

With great good fortune, I am assigned to the rock wall detail with Jay.

As we grub around on our hands and knees, carving at the rocky soil, digging a trough in which to lay the bottom course of stones, more optimism fills me. To physically be making a place for the wolves rather than just writing letters on their behalf—it is an immense difference, and a gratifying one. This is the easy part, it's true—the gravy, or the icing on the cake, after over twenty years of grassroots campaigning for the return of the wolves—endless pressure, ceaselessly applied. And as we swing the mauls and pickaxes, breaking through the stony crust, working our way through the soil horizon back down to a time, only a few inches beneath the surface, when wolves ran free in this country, I think what a pleasure it is to finally have the opportunity to be working with something real—a rock wall—as opposed to the intangible and the imagined: the dream of wolves returning. It is nothing less than therapy for cynicism and burnout.

Several times our crew takes water breaks under the autumn sun, but Jay just keeps on swinging away. From the shade of a juniper, Jerry observes, "Jay, you're a human backhoe."

We could get by without the rock walls. We could bring in a cement mixer and pour molds. But Tom Savage likes the look of stone. He's building the pens so that they can be disassembled in twelve years—the end of the project, at which point the Mexican wolves will be, we hope, fully recovered. All that will remain will be these stone walls outcropping along the hillside, like the ruins from some cliff-dwelling culture centuries ago.

It becomes quickly evident that Jay has an aptitude—no, a genius—for working with stone as well as wood. From the pile of chaotic rubble, he can select the very one needed to make the perfect fit, the only fit. Sometimes he stands there for long moments staring at the rubble pile before making his selection. Slowly, the rock wall takes beautiful shape, like the backbone of a thing emerging, and on our breaks we all gather around just to stare at the wall, like I stared the night before at the carvings, and to watch Jay work; and the thought occurs to me (made more real perhaps by the sun and dust and fatigue) that Jay is some kind of shaman who has come from who-knows-where to help put the finishing touches on that which came so very close to blinking out entirely.

It's a pleasure to go down into the arroyo and select rocks—the perfect stones—for Jay. There are halite crystals scattered all about the slope, glittering in the bronze October sunlight like spilled diamonds. It's fun, picking and choosing for Jay's work up on the hill. Which rock was upheaved to the surface, up through the crust, or scoured down to be revealed—which rock, squarish, large, level—as if all along it had been waiting to be summoned or resummoned for making one of the walls of captivity, by which the wolves can then acquire their freedom?

Andesite, diorite, granite, limestone. In some of the blocks of limestone there are fossils—fenestrellids and horn corals—from the Ordovician era, roughly half a billion years ago.

I walk down a sand creek, searching, intent on providing the artist above with the best material. The empty creek bed is a fault line, with white granite on one side and dark basalt on the other. Down its center runs a river of black sand—dissolving and disintegrating particles of basalt. I reach down and pick up a handful and enjoy the pleasant sensation of letting it sift through my fingers, each sand grain of equal size. In the heat and sun when I squint it looks like a river of black lava, on the move once again. The halite crystals throw tiny rainbow prisms of light across the hillside. Could these crystals catch sunlight in such a manner and focus as to magnify sunlight to flames, bringing about an incandescence this land has been too long without?

More rocks: heavy ones, with which to stagger back up the hill.

Jay keeps working. Tom Savage mixes mortar for him in a wheelbarrow. The sun grows fierce. Such harsh country, and without the sanctuary of winter—twelve-month access to humans; open to those who love the idea of wolves, but open also to those who hate or are afraid of the idea of wolves. A honeybee lands on the damp gray mortar and sucks at it, trying to glean what moisture it can.

"Jay," says Tom, "it is an honor to mix concrete for you."

Above us rise eroded cliff sections, partitioned by erosion into blocks and columns, so that the cliffs ringing this little valley appear to be a whole mountain's worth of perfectly ordered rock wall, built by some culture and civilization infinitely greater and vaster than we are, and long before our time—though today, at least, Jay is their equal.

We stand mesmerized again by the beauty of the tiny wall, breathing in the delicious odor of freshly mixed concrete. A lone raven calls on the wind and circles above us as if it knows what we are up to, and what we are waiting for.

"It's so beautiful," says a volunteer.

"And functional," says Tom, pausing to mop his brow. "What's more beautiful than functional?"

We push on. These walls will be here a hundred years from now, long after the fences have been disassembled. The walls will be like the echo to this story. Whether the wolves succeed in their freedom or fail, I have the urge to place a talisman of some sort in the mortar for the wolves, between the seams of stone—to at least carve a little set of pawprints in the concrete before it dries—but the heat and the rigor drain the impulse, dissipate quickly the shimmering romanticism, and besides, there's no longer any need for symbolism: the real thing is coming, due here in five weeks.

I descend into the arroyo for more stone. Tom eyes me and cautions me to take lots of water breaks. (The students and volunteers have been putting away about eight quarts a day, *each*.) Earlier in the project there was a volunteer out here who went into a hypoglycemic swoon and fell backward onto a cactus. She's okay now. Tom Savage screened all the volunteers over the phone—more than a hundred of them—and tried to weed out as many as he could. No families with kids. No dogs. No weirdos.

Dennis is swinging the pickax again, glancing at his watch frequently. "I hate it when you swing the pick and it bounces back farther than it goes in," he says.

"Be glad you're not working with Mister Punjar," says Linsey—her name for the javelinlike rock bar with which the stony crust is battered relentlessly in our efforts to set the high fence posts.

"Pretty glamorous, isn't it?" says Tom.

Andrea nods. "It really is. This is going to church for me."

Down in the bottom of one of the pens, toting another rock, I find a strange thing: a gleaming, translucent deposit of travertine—crystallized calcium carbonate, like a stalactite—with a glittering geode set in its center. With its coils and loops and folds, it looks precisely like a crystallized coyote turd—and even more strange, resting right next to it is the real thing: a slender little bleached coyote scat, wrapped with deer hair.

Its placement couldn't be unintentional. It couldn't be random. It's a fine little work of art, and too bad, I think, that the artist will be asked to give up a bit of his territory in the coming days.

Needless to say, it's been hard on Tom Savage as a contractor working with unskilled laborers. Showing us, for example, how to use a plumb bob, how to run a string-level. A walkie-talkie crackles on his hip—a volunteer is needed over on another detail, farther up the hill—and Tom points to Toni and says, "You're off to greener pastures."

One of the things that most pleases Tom about the project is the cost savings. Without wages and insurance and taxes and such, the pens are going to get built for about $150,000. A set of five nearly identical pens, built by the government, he says, cost about five hundred thousand. And the halfway houses at Sevilleta are running out of space as the wolves keep breeding.

In these politically ferocious times, with various projects being proposed for funding by one party only to be axed by the other, it's critical, says Keith, to have a bare-bones budget—something that won't draw attention to itself flying beneath radar, as it were. A budget so lean it's not even worth cutting. A budget you can't say no to.

In his second year of AmeriCorps volunteerism, Keith is maybe now the third-in-charge of things: the main man on the ground for Dave Parsons and Wendy Brown.

He's getting a lesson in rock labor, a lesson in wolf ecology, and a lesson in American politics.

"Just think," Jerry Scoville says, "we spent all that money getting rid of them, then we spent all this money bringing them back."

That night at the campfire I ask Jay why he's working so hard: why he keeps reenlisting. He shrugs. His reticence acts as a screen, it seems, for the release of raw honesty.

"I've always been for the endangered wild things," he says. "If something was hurt, I'd want to protect it." He tells us that when he was little, six or seven, some boys were running a lawn mower over lizards in the tall grass, and he was running along behind them, trying to gather up the pieces, to take care of them—the three-legged lizards, cut and gashed. He shakes his head. "I've always liked the idea of a place where something wouldn't be disturbed," he says.

How bizarre, it seems to me, that some of the students and volunteers hadn't even been born yet when these last wolves—or rather their ancestors, their progenitors—were gathered from the wild.

Around the firelight, and beneath the southern stars, and with the large tents set up bone-white all around us, it feels as if we could be on another continent, and once again, amid such youth and hope, and in the relaxation following the day's good rock work, I allow myself the luxury of optimism, despite the odds.

It's a strange, altered country the wolves will be coming back to, but perhaps they will be plastic enough to adapt, and good or lucky enough to seek out, like fingers of fire, those places on the land that are still healthy and have not been overgrazed, overmined, overlogged. Maybe there will be just enough few wild pockets and corners left to start over with.

Things are so different from when they went away. Across the valley lies the immensity of the Trinity Missile Site, where the world's first atomic bomb was exploded—a vast, shimmering, crackling expanse of land set off limits to the public forever. A huge piece of land—gone.

Just to the north lies the Bosque del Apache National Wildlife Refuge—a desert wetlands along the Rio Grande, a staging ground for the spectacle of North American bird migration: a scene, a sight, to rival Africa's, in some respects.

A strange country, and troubled times. Tomorrow morning, Tom tells us, a farmer from Idaho will be flying into the Bosque in one of those ultralight crafts, not unlike the legend of Icarus, showing the world's last remaining young whooping cranes how and where to migrate. Another little plane will be following them to help keep golden eagles off their tail: trying to escort the cranes—as if they are lost—to freedom and the future.

"They're just one oil spill away from extinction," Tom Savage says, and I think again of the lone woodland caribou that drifts in and out of my valley, up north. Noah's Ark, Ted's ark; why do all stories repeat themselves?

Strange country, strange times. I saw the black U.S. military helicopters myself, out at the Albuquerque airport. Some right-wingers have long believed that these are secret United Nations helicopters whose purpose is to spy on the comings and goings of the general American public. One can imagine their alarm, then, when earlier this fall Ted Turner recently gave a billion dollars to the United Nations. Our own country's bomber pilots cruise low over these very hills on training runs—silent black planes with outstretched wings, bellies skimming the ground, practicing flying beneath radar. Nearly everyone who's spent any time in the desert has a story of being surprised by a bomber's silent approach from over a ridge behind them, the pilot grinning down from his cockpit, close enough to hit with a rock. Now the air force is training German pilots to fly various planes and jets. People are grumbling—skittery, nervous, understanding little of it, fearing most of it. Never mind that Turner has given away a third of his wealth to try to help the environment globally—that the money was not for war, or the military; people are still spooked. Even if all our stories do repeat themselves, our imaginations are immense.

"He's at the can't-miss stage of his career," Tom Savage says—who, incidentally, asked Turner for a significant pay cut after getting the job, since it wouldn't be right for him to be working at full wages while everyone else was volunteering. "If he buys stock in something, the value jumps up 25 percent, just because he bought it."

Tom tells the volunteers again how proud he is of what they're doing, and how whether they know it now or not, they'll each take away different lessons with them, which they'll somehow be able to use, again and again, later in life. No one knows what those lessons will be, he says—but you can't work this hard and not come away with something.

THE
ANARCHIST

The anarchist, Dave Foreman, is busy on the run between
lobbying trips in D.C. and San Francisco, and preparing to
take off on an eleven-day rafting trip.

The anarchist is only one of several members of the board
of directors of the Sierra Club—though he opposed the club's

positions on both a zero-timber-harvest policy in national forests, which it endorses, and continued logging of the Tongass National Forest in Alaska, which it claims it can "live with." Another organization in which he is enmeshed is the Wildlands Project, a truly visionary and necessary blueprint that calls for restoring the wild ecosystems all around the country and linking them back together with managed corridors, as they were once connected. It is nothing less than a job-creating plan to restore ecological health and vibrancy to a nation. It is a mandate to recover the biological identity—the wildness, inherent in the soil—of the entire North American continent.

The Wildlands Project—and the anarchist—are in favor of Mexican wolf reintroduction.

The anarchist is a liberal populist with his roots so deep in traditional West Texas Anglo conservative ranching stock that he will never be able to entirely shake that legacy, nor would I want him to. It gives him an earthy authority when arguing about matters of the soil. It gives him an authority to speak for wildness that is not compromised but rather alloyed by his compassion for other rural working men and women, and their communities.

He cofounded Earth First! over twenty years ago and is only now crawling out from under that legacy; he was busted by the FBI and put on a severe probation that ended just last autumn, on his fiftieth birthday.

He looks older than fifty, but his blue eyes are gentle, his smiles and laughs genuine—he looks more thoughtful, more interested, than perhaps he used to be in holding and examining two opposing ideas at once.

We're not out in his beloved red-rock desert country, nor are we gathered around a campfire on some canyon's sandbar listening to river music and smoking cigars and sipping whiskey. We're meeting instead—Dennis Sizemore and Dave Foreman and I—at a waffle-house kind of place back in Albuquerque. It's called the Owl Cafe, and is smack in the middle of about four different strip-mall shopping centers. The establishment itself is a large sand-colored stucco building whose exterior is sculpted into the shape of an owl; we are eating in the belly of the bird. It's a Saturday morning, and it's the kind of place where parents bring their children—who are all around us in abundance, shrieking and wrestling with their Friendly Face Pancakes and Baby Burritos. The restaurant is squirming with life, with the beginning curl of the century's next wave—the mass of it coming so quickly—and for a brief moment I am rattled, picturing all of us, the collective mass of us, gnawing not on Friendly Face Pancakes but on each other, when we have run out of wild places or paved them all over and have no means of regaining or even observing balance and peace and serenity and order. Suddenly, here in the Owl, the Wildlands Project does not seem revolutionary or visionary but instead only necessary, and perhaps not quite enough.

Foreman's got about a hundred irons in the fire, and looks fresher now that the feds are off his back. I don't mean to say he looks less passionate. He still looks and speaks and acts like the man who wrote in his 1991 book *Confessions of an Eco-Warrior*:

> "Why shouldn't I be emotional, angry, passionate? Madmen and mad women are wrecking this beautiful, blue-green living Earth. Fiends who hold nothing of value but a greasy

dollar bill are tearing down the pillars of evolution building for nearly four thousand million years. . . .

"We are told that the Gray Wolf and Grizzly Bear are gone from most of the West and can never be restored, that the Elk and Bison and Panther are but shades in the East and will not come back, that Glen Canyon and Hetch Hetchy are beneath dead reservoir water and we shall never see them again, that the Tall Grass Prairie and Eastern Deciduous Forest are only memories and that we can never have big wilderness east of the Rockies again.

"Bunk!"

The anarchist is talking about the militias—many of whose members utter the same quotes by Thomas Jefferson and Thomas Paine that the anarchist has used in his discussions of freedom, wildness, and liberty. He can still crank up the passion, the outrage—referring to the county commissioners and other corporate-bought politicians who oppose Mexican wolf recovery as "the lapdogs of the right-wingers who do not represent the scientific consensus.

"We need more local folks who are willing to stand up," the anarchist says. He's been in the rural communities all his life and has known all along what the polls are only just now certifying—that the majority of these communities want the wildlands protected, want the wolves and grizzlies and bison to return, and are just not being given voice, or are being made timid by the stridency of the "lapdogs" of industry.

The anarchist sips his coffee, looks out the window as if trying consciously to calm his throbbing heart: as if magma is surging through his body. He rests a moment longer, looks back at us, and begins talking, with enthusiasm, about beavers.

There used to be beavers all over the Great Basin, he says. He tells us about a pilot project in southern Utah that will attempt to use beavers to restore a river course devastated by overgrazing and fire suppression, which has allowed the exotic tamarisk plant—unpalatable to damn near everything, but especially to beavers—to replace the native willows.

There's nothing but sagebrush and tamarisk around the sloughing, eroding banks of the creek now. The plan, Foreman says, is to bring in some beavers, which will begin doing what beavers do—making dams—which will displace the river's energies into backwaters, creating wetlands in which willows can then grow.

Foreman calls them "kamikaze beavers" because they'll have to build their dams out of sagebrush, which won't be nutritious enough to carry them through the winter. That first generation of beavers will probably starve, but they'll have repaired the hydrology enough so that once again willows and cottonwoods (which beavers need to survive) can regenerate and flourish in the shallow standing water of the backwashes, thereby ensuring a food source and survival for the next wave or generation of beavers. It reminds me of "Turner's wolves." I picture the beaver's, the cottonwood's, the willow's return as being yet another story of weaving: the next century's story of sewing back together.

The anarchist smiles, picturing the straight-line gully route of a degraded stream curling back into the supple, sinuous curves of its origin and innate desire.

"Does the beaver need the willows, or do the willows need the beaver?" he asks.

"We've screwed up the ecosystem," the anarchist says, speaking of the entire desert Southwest. "We don't even know what the lobo is supposed to do in the system," he says, explaining that we so quickly eradicated the wolf's native prey base—the Merriam's elk, deer, pronghorns, and bighorns being hunted nearly to extinction to feed the mining camps of the late 1800s—that we're faced with a piece of "missing history."

"We're traveling with ecological ignorance," he says, "but there's certainly no reason to continue in that direction. We don't know what the natural system was like. We're trying to put together a jigsaw puzzle we've never even seen," he says, referring again to the broken, fractured landscape of the Southwest.

"We can let the wolf show us," he says, with satisfaction.

There are other story writers on his mind—the paths of jaguars, ocelots, condors returning to their native land, their paths weaving back across this diminishing wild country—but the wolf is one of the widest ranging of all mammals, a great one to start with, if you want to begin reading the stories of that "missing history" and listening—for once—to what the land and its other components desire.

We go outside into the bright warm spring air and say our good-byes. Dennis is headed back to Salt Lake to do more of his eternal paperwork, and the anarchist, whose work I respect immensely but who has not yet agreed with me that my wild valley upon the Canadian line, the Yaak, is ecologically worthy of being a wilderness cornerstone of the Wildlands Project, prepares for his raft trip.

I head north, from the southern tip of the West to my home at the northern tip. It's not that far a journey.

It feels crooked, confusing. I'm leaving behind a somewhat protected primitive area in the Blue Mountains, where there are not any wolves that we know of—and heading to a place, the Yaak, that has no protected wilderness, but has wild wolves living in it. It seems as if the Blues have the paper on which to tell the story, but no pen, while the Yaak has both pen and paper—though even as that story is being written, the paper, the surface on which the story can be told, is being shredded.

On the plane, headed home, I look down at the beautiful crenulations on the dry red land below—the writhings and contortions, the folds and sinuosities of the canyons.

Everything writes sentences: rivers, streams, wind currents, elk herds, migrating geese, wolves. Everything has a voice. Some voices are merely less audible than others. We ignore them at our peril; in shunning the lessons of history we embrace ignorance, we fail to take advantage of guidelines for the future. Our stories, our lives, our cultures sag and fracture into gibberish and monosyllabic chants of More, more, more. Like the beavers starving on sage and tamarisk, we are running out of the thing that once sustained us: a certain spirit and imagination upon the land, and certain stories told to us by that land.

A gulf exists between the captive wolves and their native landscape, just as one exists between us and our future relationship to that land.

I wish them luck. I wish all of us luck.

CLOSER

In December I return to Ted Turner's ranch to watch the Round River students watch the wolves' return, or to watch them return halfway. The chances are long that these particular wolves will ever make it all the way into the woods. The wolves that will be chosen for next year's release will be coming from the halfway house at Sevilleta. These wolves coming into Turner's ranch are like an echo of those wolves slated for the wild. Out at Turner's ranch, the students and volunteers have finished all but one pen. The first group of wolves has already been paired up in Pens Four and Five, and two other pairs are coming tonight, riding in the back of pickup trucks in dog kennels. The portable kennels have stickers on them that say WOLF: THIS SIDE UP. Two sister wolves are coming from the Wild Canid Survival and Research Center in Eureka, Missouri. Two males, brothers, are coming from the Living Desert Zoo in Carlsbad, New Mexico. All the wolves are the same age: one year, eight months.

When I drive in it's late, but all the students and volunteers are still awake, gathered around a smoke-sweet campfire of Arizona walnut, too excited to sleep: their last night on the ranch. The wolves are already up on the hill in their kennels, awaiting release into the pens early the next morning. It's cold, in the twenties; a couple of inches of snow fell yesterday.

There is for everyone an unspoken awareness that tomorrow is the payoff for all that has come before, that three and a half months of work have yielded the right, the privilege, of tomorrow's glimpse. The students sit with great ease and pleasure and an earned, comfortable anticipation. We talk far into the night, drinking cup after cup of tea, edging closer and closer to the campfire as the chill of night draws around.

Since I've last seen Jay, he has carved more veins into the leaves on which his frog is resting. It looks so real that when I see it, I comment, "That sombitch is ready to jump," as if it awaits now only the permission of Jay, its creator, to launch itself from that walnut branch. You can see the individual stomata in the leaf. It looks like and has to it the feel, I think, the aura, of the kind of thing pharaohs used to be buried with back in pyramid days. Jay admits that it's been kind of slow going the last several weeks: that this is the part of the carving where it's hard to tell if you're making any progress.

When we ask him what's the hardest thing he's ever carved, he thinks for a while and then decides that it was the horned lizards. We groan, imagining the intricacies of those ancient, desert-sculpted creatures, and Jay tells us that he carved a baby horned lizard, too, with its mama—more groans—but that what was really hard was carving the tiny ants that the little horned lizard was eating.

A brilliant sunrise, the world sheeted in frost. We finish our breakfast of tea and oatmeal, and start up the dry canyon in single file. We'll ease up over the stony bluff, gather around the observation booth on the ridge a few hundred yards away, and watch Jay and Tom release the four new wolves into the two new pens: one Eureka female with one Carlsbad male in both Pen Two and Pen Three. These wolves have been selected for genetic redundancy so that if they vanish, they will not represent a loss to the genetic variability of the world's tiny population. Computer dating.

Anything for freedom. Anything for hope, for a chance.

A canyon wren sings to us as we travel up the cobble-strewn canyon, passing between the hulks of leafless cottonwoods, the dried brown and yellow leaves rustling against our boots. At one point we must leap across a wide stretch of stream, and we stumble with early-morning awkwardness and stiff, cold feet across

that mossy, loose-rock crossing, splashing and clattering like cattle. We bushwhack through a copse of drying cattails, and plumes
of cattails explode in puffs skyward, floating seeds spiraling upward.
We're all coated instantly with seed wrack, and cloaked in gold
light, as the fine drift of cattail puff glows incandescent. Seeds in
our hair, on our arms and coats, clinging to our boots: the agents
of dispersal. We push on up the canyon, a part of the landscape,
carrying those seeds to new crevices, new veins of soil.

   We ascend to the backside of the ridge and peer down.
The pens look as if they have been there forever. The rusting wire
fences are nearly invisible, as Tom Savage had planned and
hoped. Built into the hillside, the neat stone walls are pleasing:
they do not disrupt the view; they do not disrupt anything. We
gather around like a little clan, cold in the ridge's wind, and wait
in umber light. The wind is strong from the north.

   I'm not aware of worshiping individual animals or
species. My affinity, my allegiance, is with complete landscapes,
with wild places. I'd rather try to protect an undesignated wilderness area—a landscape's wild qualities, which comprises millions
of variables—than spend energy on lobbying for the return of
some single species—a grizzly, a caribou, a wolf. You could go out
and buy a wolf and set it down in some lacking landscape, but the
next morning the landscape's problems would still be the same.
You can travel up to Canada or Alaska and capture one of the
wild things in that country and bring it down to some other
place, as if shopping to fill in the emotional blanks of a fractured
landscape. Yet you would have changed nothing of substance, but
merely gratified yourself; the land itself—the wild land—remains
imperiled.

That said, I am not prepared for what I feel when I see the wolves enter—or reenter—their new world.

Jay swings open the gate to one of the portable kennels and a wolf glides out like smoke, as real, as vital, as any animal I have ever seen. I wonder, is it my imagination or has the compression of a race, a subspecies, down to these last hundred-plus individuals somehow imbued each one with an increased density of spirit, increased responsibility? Nothing less than two million years of carving rest on this wolf, and a few others, this bright winter day.

The yellow-green eyes of fire catch the sunlight and glow. It's a Carlsbad male, that's out first. Even though he's a bit soft looking, not yet possessing the electric muscle tone of a creature living in the wild, he's one of the most beautiful animals I've ever seen. We stare at him with nothing less than hunger, watching every move: the confidence of each joint's articulation, the confidence of muzzle taking in new scent; the confidence of being alive in the world.

Those yellow-green eyes: everything they have is in those eyes, as you or I might pack everything we have into a storage shed, or the back of a truck. Their eyes carry more than ours do. We are children looking into those eyes—we have been here such a short time, while they have been here so long. Who are we, to consider saving them?

The male trots immediately toward the fence, makes a couple of passes up and down it, then crouches and relieves himself.

The female comes out. She's sprier, wilder—she flares from the handlers, skitters away as if windblown. She makes straight for the place that the male scent marked, pauses, then begins digging at that spot and sniffing at it. Later she will rub her back against the place, as if she cannot get enough of that soil.

The other two are released into Pen Three. The male comes right on out, but the female won't exit, even when her kennel is picked up and held open over the ground—as if someone is trying to shake out the last kernels of popcorn from a paper bag. She won't come out; she has all four legs braced against the inside of the kennel's walls. Again the kennel is shaken, held upside down, and finally she skirts out and runs promptly for the pen's boundaries.

Such avoidance behavior—especially coming from the females—is pleasing to all. They will teach it to their pups.

For the next hour and a half we watch the wolves explore their new homes. The couple in Pen Two—downwind from the other wolves—seem more comfortable with their enclosure as well as each other; soon they are playing together: crouching, pouncing, teasing.

The couple in Pen Three, however, appear more tense. Smack in front of us the physical evidence of recombination, but with such varying, seemingly random responses. Pen One, frisky; Pen Three, tense.

The weight of responsibility begins to settle with something closer to its full import. Humans will be doing the weaving and reweaving for a little while—helping set back in motion that which we nearly extinguished.

Jerry Scoville is transfixed with his binoculars, as are all the students.

"Just think," he says quietly, "nearly every dog in the world comes from that one creature." He nods down at the wolves, which are still examining their new quarters with ceaseless curiosity. This is the ultimate contract, Jerry says. In one sense, we have sculpted dogs from the rootstock of wolves: French poodles, Jack Russell terriers, black Labs. In the larger, longer scale, though, wolves have been sculpting us, the space for us, and the idea of us—a creature that desires loyalty—since before we even arrived.

I'm aware that we are the ones who are doing the weaving—choosing which new wolf to recombine with which other one—but up here on the bluff, with their graceful movements holding us spellbound, it seems as though surely the wolves are in charge. Wherever they go, whatever they do, we are going to watch them; we cannot look away.

The male in Pen Two again squats and urinates on a patch of open soil near the fence; the female soon wanders over to investigate that spot, digs there for a while, then writhes in the soil at that spot. That new spot.

Jets of cold morning frost-breath leap from all four wolves' mouths as they pace. Small birds—we can't identify what kind—flock toward the junipers as if to greet the wolves and then swirl away. Next spring perhaps those birds' nests will be lined with tufts of wolf fur.

Whenever the wolves stop pacing for a moment—to follow with their eyes the nimbus of passing birds; to study the sky for the source of a lone raven's croak—they seem to vanish: the color of the wheat-toned grama grass on the hillside is still the exact hue of their coats, painted in that rich coppery light. In their twenty-two years of captivity, they have not lost this.

From behind the next ridge, over in Pen Four, one of the other wolves—knowing surely of their arrival, despite being upwind—begins to howl. When he first cuts loose it startles the little female in Pen One, makes her flinch.

As we listen to that howl echo off the rock bluffs—the Howler carries on for eight minutes, punctuating his howls with barks—there is no one among us now who does not believe the wolves will make it.

Later, the female in Pen Two pauses at the eastern edge of the pen and looks up at the twelve-foot fence; crouches as if to jump, coils like a spring and stares up at the top—but she does not attempt it.

Yet for those few seconds that she was poised like that, there was such a confidence in her body that I believe had she tried it, she would have made it. It would have been a phenomenal leap. But she had me believing. The beauty of her had me believing.

Too soon, it's time to leave. We've drunk in the sight of them. An hour and a half has passed like a blink. We slide back down over the ridge and leave them to themselves, such as the fences will allow.

Walking back in that December sunshine, it seems so easy.

I have in my pocket the sun-bleached half husk of an Arizona walnut, taken from the creek below where the wolves will be living for the next year. The half husk is smooth as bone, and as pale; the nut's grooves and striations have all but been worn away by the force of running water. The seed, the nutmeat, has been hollowed out long ago, leaving only open cavities, like the eye sockets in a desert-bright skull, or the place where hip attaches to a pelvis—like the replica of a part of a tiny skeleton, carved and polished by some sublime craftsman.

What tree would this husk have grown into, had it found purchase in fertile soil rather than being tumbled down a rocky wash? Where is its other half? What seeds of recombination—what instructions, what blueprints—once existed within it?

I like how smooth the half husk is when I reach in my pocket and find it there. I like how everything's starting over: the courage of that art. The husk reminds me that they're halfway there. No one knows for sure which direction they'll go—vanishing to history, or recovering and stepping brightly into the future. I know only that regardless of which direction they take, they are now halfway there.

SNOW

Eleven of them were chosen from Sevilleta for freedom.
A pair of adults—proven breeders, mates from the year
before—were delivered to the acclimation pen at the Turkey
Creek site, the southernmost site, and at the lowest elevation
(around 6,000 feet)—in late January. And another pair, along

with a female yearling, were delivered (also in late January) to the Campbell Blue site.

In early February, the third and largest pack—a mated pair, two yearling females, and two male pups—was transferred to the Hawk's Nest site.

All three sites were constructed within the Apache National Forest.

Like some roll of the dice, that was the manner in which they would be cast out, or spilled out, onto the land: two, three, and six.

Upon the wolves' release, our questions focused narrowly, winnowing quickly the previous eighteen years of conjecture.

Would they stay in the areas where they'd been released?

Would they dig dens, become pregnant, and whelp pups?

Would there be trouble with livestock?

Would they be able to teach themselves to hunt (as the reintroduced captive-bred red wolves have done in the Southeast), or would the government be assisting them with the dropped carcasses of road-killed elk, deer, antelope, and javelina forever: a kind of eternally burning Olympic flame of supplemental feeding?

Back at Sevilleta, these same wolves had killed small mammals and birds that had blundered into their pens, including the ravens that were always trying to steal their food.

An Interagency Field Team was assigned to coordinate the project from this point. Alan Armistad, a Mexican wolf specialist with the U.S. Department of Agriculture's Wildlife Services, would be responsible for dealing with any livestock depredation; Diane Boyd-Heger would be the wolf biologist representing the Arizona Department of Game and Fish; and Wendy Brown, the wolf biologist, would be representing the U.S. Fish & Wildlife Service.

For about two months, the eleven wolves hung out in the little one-third-acre acclimation pens, settling in to the sights and sounds and odors of the new place, becoming accustomed to the colder air and the scent of the new forest. (The two northernmost packs—the Hawk's Nest Six and Campbell Blue Unmated-Two-Plus-One—were up around 8,000 feet, in spruce and fir.)

Volunteers and team research personnel camped in the vicinity, out of sight, watching the wolves during this period. In speaking with them, I have the sense that they were doing something much more than watching: being there for the wolves as both witnesses and protectors during the waiting-on period. The biologists can't really discuss this kind of stuff—the press and especially the ranchers would rip them to shreds—but I get the sense that there was an intangible exchange going on between the wolves and their guardians camped not far away: the biologists rarely if ever were seen by the wolves, but the wolves knew that the guardians were there. And the wolves understood some new things about humanity, I would hope and suspect, across that distance.

Wendy Brown says that originally the biologists had hoped to set up camps at a distance from which they might be able to occasionally peek over a ridge and observe the wolves, but that proved impossible. The wolves always knew when they were being watched; they always spotted the watchers watching them.

So the researchers moved back—they widened the gap, as if already giving the wolves a kind of release, or freedom. And

I thought again of Jerry Scoville's comment about the "ultimate contract" forged between humans and wolves so long ago: even all the way back, perhaps, to the time when stars were first exploding, and the orbits of things—the followers, and the followed—were being suggested, and then decided on.

All our science and telemetry; all our careful, intelligent planning and management; all our good intent and efforts were still unable, or unwilling—for the procedure would have been too invasive—to broach one of the most basic of mysteries: were any of the three adult pairs of wolves pregnant?

"Possibly," said Wendy Brown. "Possibly."

The gates to the acclimation pens were opened on Sunday, March 29, during a big snowstorm. Some of the wolves chose freedom completely and instantly, while others chose it more cautiously, seeming to consider the pros and cons. But by the following morning, they had all chosen freedom, and already the snow was beginning to erase the signature, the sentences, of their choice and their direction.

Science picked up the narrative, of course. Telemetry indicated that all the wolves had ventured roughly a mile from their acclimation pens, with the Turkey Creek pair—the proven breeders, and familiar mates—confident enough, it seemed, to have split up for a little while, which is normal behavior for members of a pack, as they explored their new surroundings.

The Turkey Creek pair went back toward their pen a couple of days later, to finish eating one of the road-killed deer that the biologists had left there.

◆ ◆ ◆

The Campbell Blue Three and Hawk's Nest Six moved still a little farther from their pens, and then each pack settled in a fixed area for twenty-four and forty-eight hours, respectively.

"This suggests they've explored their surroundings and found areas they're currently content with. Behaviorally, this is very encouraging," said Wendy Brown. It was *possible* this was pre-denning behavior.

Another six inches of snow fell in the north country, on the Campbell Blue Three and the Hawk's Nest Six. The snow held their tracks briefly, then dissolved.

The team went in and closed the gates on all the acclimation pens so that if the wolves did begin to dig dens, they wouldn't be tempted to do so back in their pens.

On gate-closing day, the Campbell Blue Three howled and followed the researchers all the way back to their old acclimation pen and watched unseen (but monitored by the telemetry equipment) as the workers closed the gate for good.

Down south, the Turkey Creek pair found a lion hunter's camp and began harassing the hunter's dogs that were staked in camp. It seemed as if the wolves were in some kind of rush to lay down claim to their territory—the terms of their freedom—and had immediately found the "interlopers": as if no time had passed at all, since they, or their kind, were last here. The lion hunter wasn't too happy about it, but he moved his camp.

The Campbell Blue Three were seen on the highway a couple of times, and, to the concern of the biologists, did not

appear especially spooked. One time the wolves ran away immediately when sighted, but another time they stopped and stared
back, which is fine as long as they don't ever stop and stare back
at someone who's willing to risk the jail term and $100,000 fine
for shooting them. Wendy Brown mentioned that aversive con-
ditioning might be considered if an appropriate opportunity pre-
sented itself: firecrackers, perhaps, or some other sort of hazing.
The good news was that the Campbell Blue Three were hanging
out up high in big-time elk country—grassy meadows and old,
open Ponderosa pine forests.

All three packs were howling—lacing, crafting the ten-
tative boundaries of their new territories with their travels, and
with their howls, and their scat, building a thing as real as Jay
Nochta's stone wall, but as invisible as hope.

In mid-April, a member of the field team saw the Hawk's
Nest Six chasing an adult elk. The wolves appeared to have just
sort of blundered on to the elk, and started chasing it, which is
pretty much the way biologists figured things would work, at
first. The wolves may know instinctively, as individuals, how to
kill, but there might be some fine tuning to do with regard to
hunting and working as a team.

No evidence of a subsequent kill could be found—the
researchers kept watching the sky for the signature, *ravens*, but saw
none—though some of the wolves' scats were showing rabbit hair,
indicating the wolves were already doing some hunting in the
wild. The recovery team had cut the wolves' supplemental diet of
road-kill back to about 50 percent of what they'd need to survive

in the long term. They were tightening the screws, if indeed any were loose in the first place, after only twenty-two years.

Six days later, a husband and wife were driving back from town to their ranch when they saw three members of the big Hawk's Nest pack chasing an adult elk, which appeared weak and distressed, possibly wounded. The wolves chased the elk into a creek.

It was evening—almost dusk—and the ranchers left, to avoid disturbing the wolves. And because they did not have a phone out at their ranch, they drove all the way back to a pay phone and reported the incident.

The next day recovery team members went out and found the dead elk—an old cow—completely submerged, but much consumed nonetheless: the first confirmed kill. As best as the biologists could tell, the wolves—a yearling female and the two male pups—had not been able to pull the elk out of the creek, so they had had to dive down beneath the surface to rip off a chunk of elk and then eat it underwater, or swim back to shore and chow down on it there before swimming back out into the creek and submerging for more.

The water roiling, and the color of it staining red, then pink.

These were the same wolves that some of us had been doubting, worrying that they might not know what it would take to survive.

The field team pulled the elk out of the water so the wolves could get to it more easily (though who knows; perhaps they liked having it underwater, so that the ravens could not get to it), and pulled one of the elk's teeth to help determine its age and general health.

The next day, five of the Hawk's Nest Six were observed feasting on the carcass. It seemed they might as well have never been away, that the world had never missed them.

There's not enough data to even begin a conclusion yet, but perhaps the new literature is already being written—or rather, perhaps we are already discovering some old stories: old land-literature, old wolf-literature. Wolves in the far north often endeavor to chase their prey out onto the ice of ponds and lakes, where the prey's power is more easily neutralized; it's possible a similar instinct rests buried within each cell of the Mexican wolves—the urge to haze their prey into the water. It does not seem unlikely, though in the scant literature that exists regarding wild Mexican wolves, I've never seen this strategy discussed.

We know nothing. It's possible we know less than nothing: that we have busied ourselves knowing the wrong things, and have built our beliefs and values on old inaccuracies while failing to observe vanishing truths.

It's staggering to me to think that nonetheless we're going to get a second chance.

Were any of the three pairs of adults pregnant? Eleven could become twenty or thirty overnight. The way you go to bed one warm breezy night in the spring and then wake up in the morning, and every bud in the forest, it seems, has opened to new leaves as you slept; and something new is in the air, some vigor and odor and feeling, as a result. Something we can't prove is "good," but that we know is good, strong, healthy, and right. Something pleasing to the eyes, and to the soul, and to the heart, and to the land. Something necessary, year after year.

The same April, I was back down in Texas. I took a drive out to where Wolf Corner had once been—the place where on our Sunday drives my family and I had sometimes seen the wolves hanging on the fence.

The grassland was all gone. In its place was a vast shopping center, flanked by miles of strip malls, and a sea of concrete. It seemed longer ago than thirty years. I walked out into the parking lot to the place where I estimated the hanging fence had once been. I tapped the concrete with my foot, trying to summon some lost spirits, though I heard and felt none.

It was windy, and there was an empty flagpole over by one of the stores, with the flagless chainsteel halyard banging against the flagpole. It was making an insistent, clanging, hollow sound. I tapped the concrete again with my foot. A woman went walking past with a big bag of groceries. She clicked an electronic beeper to unlock her car door, climbed in, and drove away.

I tried to imagine, and measure, the distance between her, between us, and those wolves diving down under the water in the creek to tear loose pieces of their new kill, in their new land, but I could not. It seemed like two different stories, though I knew it wasn't. There was still, just barely and now for a while longer, enough room in the world for both.

BEGINNING

Just as one story's end is only another's beginning, so too do the old stories attempt, with tenacity, to retell themselves—as if to claim stubbornly their territory against the encroachment of new stories. The wolves had been free exactly one month, a full cycle of the moon, before the first one, the Turkey Creek male, was shot and killed.

Information was sketchy, but according to the USF&WS, the male, a four-year-old, got into dog trouble again, and was shot while attacking a camper's dog; while attempting to claim fully, with ferocity and time-carved uncompromising-ness, his and his mate's territory—to drive out or kill any com-peting canids. There's no telling how many coyotes the Turkey Creek pair had already killed or run out of the area.

I'm certain that a map, an overlay, rests in the stars above us—some ordered charting, some alternate plan, reflecting the topography of the country the Turkey Creek pair would have been able to roam, and would still roam, had they been "success-ful." Some different charting, where such an existence would have been possible.

But if "success" meant not obeying their identity, these wolves would have no part of it. And what good is ghost landscape, or memory, to those of us stranded below in the here and now?

If your memory could go back far enough, you might be reminded of events that had occurred only a little more than a hundred years ago, not all that far from the Blue Range. In 1893 there was a remarkable alpha male wolf in the Currumpaw region of northern New Mexico that the ranchers named Lobo, who ran with a pack of five other stock-killing wolves and whose last days were chronicled by Ernest Thompson Seton in his story, "Lobo, King of the Currumpaw."

Lobo was a giant among wolves—at 150 pounds, he would have been massive for even an Alaskan wolf—which might lead one to wonder if he wasn't a wolf-dog cross, or some now-extinct subspecies—C. l. mogollonensis, or C. l. monstrabilis, the Plains buffalo wolf—the last of his kind, perhaps, there at century's end, who might have fallen in with a pack of smaller *C. l. baileyi.*

He ran in Mexican wolf country, with what were surely one of the dying last bands of Mexican wolves. Ranchers testified that his howl was distinctive among all others, as was his cunning.

All of the wolves in Lobo's little pack seem to have been ultra-survivors—the last few having been whittled to the bitter edge of existence by the long campaign against them by the ceaseless traps and guns and poisons—and most of his pack were much larger than the typical Mexican wolf. The second-ranking male was also said to be particularly massive, though still not as immense as Lobo. Whatever their pedigree, it is all gone to dust now, and no real matter whether they were pure *C. l. baileyi,* or a cross with some other, or they were simply that big from gorging on so much livestock.

Dust from the last century. There's no telling.

Whatever the reasons for their exception, they traveled in the last of Mexican wolf country—becoming, in that manner, Mexican wolves, regardless of blood line. The old wolves—the last of the old wolves.

Also among their members was a yellow wolf of remarkable quickness, who reportedly could catch antelope for the pack; and a beautiful white wolf called Blanca—the alpha female, and Lobo's mate.

A chart of their destruction brings to mind Jerry Scoville's concept of "socially retarded wolves"—wolves whose behavior had been so shaped by the influx of livestock into their country, and by their own persecution, that what was witnessed in those times could surely have been anomalous, some alteration of the essence that was originally in them.

The Currumpaw band was keying in on livestock in those final days. They seemed to have led charmed lives, and not only evaded but scorned ranchers and their poisons. It was estimated that they killed a cow a day—nearly two thousand cattle, then, over the peak of their five-year reign. At first glance their legend seems to have to it the burnishment of myth, but it might not be all that improbable. Clearly the Currumpaw pack had learned that to avoid being poisoned they could only eat once from a kill before moving on, rather than settling in and feeding on the carcass over a course of days, as would be their "normal" behavior. Six wolves gnawing quickly at a freshly fallen cow and then running twenty miles in a night, to the next cattle herd, doesn't sound so terribly unlikely.

The pack seemed to prefer yearling heifers, and would no longer eat carrion. They didn't care for sheep, though one night in November 1893 Blanca and the yellow wolf reportedly killed 250 sheep, without eating any.

A cowboy once rode up on the wolves after they had just killed a heifer (Lobo had caught her by the neck, dug in his heels, and flipped her; then he had stood back and let the other wolves swarm her) and, shouting, the cowboy ran the wolves off and quickly laced the newly killed carcass with strychnine.

But when he returned the next morning, expecting to find dead and dying wolves scattered about, he discovered instead that the wolves had eaten the heifer, but had carefully bitten out and tossed aside the poisoned parts.

Shortly after this incident the bounty for Lobo was set at $1,000.

All manner of houndsmen and trappers pursued him, coming from all over the Southwest. The horses plunged off cliffs in the pursuit. The hounds were never seen again.

Seton, who had been a wolf hunter before becoming a writer, decided to go after Old Lobo himself. Seton rode the country, learning the routes and observing the scattered cattle skeletons left across the countryside like the driftwood spars deposited by some regular tide, and because of the ruggedness of the country, Seton soon understood that he would have to use poison and traps to kill "the old king."

"Acting on the hint of an old trapper," Seton wrote, "I melted some cheese together with the kidney fat of a freshly killed heifer, stewing it in a china dish, and cutting it with a bone knife to avoid the taint of metal. When the mixture was cool, I cut it into lumps, and making a hole in one side of each lump, I inserted a large dose of strychnine and cyanide, contained in a capsule that was impermeable by any odor; finally I sealed the holes up with pieces of the cheese itself. During the whole process, I wore a pair of gloves steeped in the hot blood of the heifer, and even avoided breathing on the baits. When all was ready, I put them in a raw-hide bag rubbed all over with blood, and rode forth dragging the liver and kidneys of the beef at the end of a rope. With this I made a ten-mile circuit, dropping a bait at each quarter of a mile, and taking the utmost care, always, not to touch any with my hands."

Seton knew that Lobo "generally" came into that area around the early part of each week, as he and his pack made the rounds of their territory. That night Seton heard Lobo's howl, and the next morning, Seton set out, eager to know the results. He soon came upon the tracks (Lobo's measured five and a half inches from claw to heel), and soon found where Lobo and his pack had followed the scent of Seton's drag toward the waiting baits.

Seton came to where he'd laid the first bait, and saw where Lobo had sniffed around it, then picked it up.

"Then I could not conceal my delight," Seton wrote. "'I've got him at last,' I exclaimed; 'I shall find him stark within a mile,' and I galloped on with eager eyes fixed on the great broad track in the dust. It led me to the second bait and that also was gone. How I exulted—I surely have him now and perhaps several of his band. But there was the broad paw-mark still on the drag; and though I stood in the stirrup and scanned the plain I saw nothing that looked like a dead wolf. Again I followed—to find now that the third bait was gone—and the king-wolf's track led on to the fourth, there to learn that he had not really taken the bait at all, but had merely carried them in his mouth. Then having piled the three on the fourth, he scattered filth over them to express his utter contempt for my devices."

Another story: Lobo and the sheep. A vast herd of sheep was kept with a half dozen goats, to help prevent stampedes. (Ordinarily, sheep stampede easily, but if they are alarmed in the presence of goats, they will instead crowd around the goats, "recognizing the superior intelligence of their bearded cousins," according to Seton, and a stampede can be avoided.)

Old Lobo went into such a herd, however, leapt into the sheep, ran across their backs—as if crossing a stream by leaping from stone to stone—killed the goats in the herd's center, and then commenced to scatter the sheep in a thousand directions.

◆ ◆ ◆

In the telltale paw prints, Seton began to notice Lobo's responses to traps, and tried to outwit him by setting traps in an "H" pattern so that when Lobo encountered the central trap in the middle of the trail and stepped to the side of it, he might catch his foot in the unscented "blind" set of another.

"Lobo came trotting along the trail, and was fairly between the parallel lines before he detected the single trap in the trail, but he stopped in time, and why or how he knew enough I cannot tell, the Angel of the wild things must have been with him, but without turning an inch to the right or left, he slowly and cautiously backed on his own tracks, putting each paw exactly in its old track until he was off the dangerous ground. Then returning at one side he scratched clods and stones with his hind feet till he had sprung every trap. This he did on many other occasions . . ."

The story gets awful now. As if again there is such resistance to any new story. As if, when you crack the surface, the old story is always the first one out, and perhaps—or so you wonder, in times of discouragement or weariness—the only story there is.

Seton caught a lucky break. He wrote that Old Lobo might still be out there with his pack "to-day, but for an unfortunate alliance that proved his ruin and added his name to the long list of heroes who, unassailable when alone, have fallen through the indiscretion of a trusted ally."

Seton noticed that one of the smaller wolves was often traveling slightly to the side of the rest of the pack, investigating things and displaying more independence. He reasoned that it was a female—believing that Lobo would not tolerate such "independence" from another male. Seton decided to go after the "exploring" wolf. He killed a heifer, and set "one or two rather obvious traps" next to it. Next he cut off the head, which the wolves never fooled with, and set it off a little ways as if it were of no importance, and then buried his two strongest traps, "deodorized and concealed with the utmost care. During my operations I kept my hands, boots, and implements smeared with fresh blood, and afterward sprinkled the ground with the same, as though it had flowed from the head; and when the traps were buried in the dust I brushed the place over with the skin of a coyote and with a foot of the same animal made a number of tracks over the traps. The head was so placed that there was a narrow passage between it and some tussocks, and in this passage I buried two of my best traps, fastening them to the head itself.

"Wolves have a habit of approaching every carcass they get the wind of, in order to examine it, even when they have no intention of eating of it, and I hoped that this habit would bring the Currumpaw pack within reach of my latest stratagem. I did not doubt that Lobo would detect my handiwork about the meat, and prevent the pack approaching it, but I did build some hopes on the head, for it looked as though it had been thrown aside as useless.

"Next morning, I sallied forth to inspect the traps, and there, oh joy! were the tracks of the pack, and the place where the beef-head and its traps had been was empty. A hasty study of the trail showed that Lobo had kept the pack from approaching the meat, but one, a small wolf, had evidently gone on to examine the head as it lay apart and had walked right into one of the traps.

"We set out on the trail, and within a mile discovered that the hapless wolf was Blanca. Away she went, however, at a gallop, and although encumbered by the beef-head, which weighted over fifty pounds, she speedily distanced my companion who was on foot. But we overtook her when she reached the rocks for the horns of the cow's head became caught and held her fast. She was the handsomest wolf I had ever seen. Her coat was in perfect condition and nearly white."

Blanca howled, caught fast, and Old Lobo answered from up on the mesa. Seton and his friends lassoed Blanca and killed her by straining their horses in opposite directions until "the blood burst from her mouth."

"Homeward then we rode," he reports, "exulting," with Old Lobo still roaring up on the mesas.

Later that night Old Lobo's howls came closer, until he reached the spot where Blanca had been killed, and "his heart-broken wailing was piteous to hear. Even the stolid cowboys noticed it, and said they had 'never heard a wolf carry on like that before.'"

That night Lobo came straight on into the ranch house and "surprised our unfortunate watch-dog outside and tore him to little bits within fifty yard of the door."

Knowing that Lobo would be reckless in his grief, Seton set traps all around his house; and in fact Lobo stepped into one of them, but "such was his strength, he had torn himself loose and cast it aside."

The story gets even worse. It reads at first as testimony to a wolf's enduring wildness, but one becomes aware soon enough of a commensurate shadow—man's obsessive opposition to such wild force.

Seton gathered every trap he could find—130 in all—and set them in groups of four at the mouth of a certain canyon Lobo used, and then on up into the canyon, fastening every one of them to a log, and burying every log.

"In burying them, I carefully removed the sod and every particle of earth that was lifted we put in blankets, so that after the sod was replaced and all was finished the eye could detect no trace of human handiwork."

Then Seton got the body of dead Blanca and dragged her all over hell and back—across the traps, and all around the ranch—and finally he cut off one of her paws and "stepped" it over each of the 130 traps.

I want to know what the scene must have looked like to someone watching from, say, the moon. Or perhaps I don't. Or perhaps the distance of those 105 years is the same distance as the moon, or some farther point.

Seton retired to bed late that night. He thought he heard Old Lobo howl once, but couldn't be sure whether it was a dream, or real.

He rode his trapline the next day but couldn't examine all 130 traps before dark.

The next day he went out again, to the far north end of the canyon, and there he found Old Lobo with each foot in a trap, "perfectly helpless," and with "numerous tracks showing how the cattle had gathered about him to insult the fallen despot, without daring to approach within his reach."

He had been in the trap two nights and two days and was worn out. "Yet, when I went near him, he rose up with bristling mane and raised his voice, and for the last time made the cañon reverberate with his deep bass roar, a call for help, the muster call of his band. But there was none to answer him, and, left alone in his extremity, he whirled about with all his strength and made a desperate effort to get at me. All in vain, each trap was a dead drag of over three hundred pounds, and in their relentless fourfold grasp, with great steel jaws on every foot, and the heavy logs and chains all entangled together, he was absolutely powerless. How his huge ivory tusks did grind on those cruel chains, and when I ventured to touch him with my rifle-barrel he left grooves on it which are there to this day. His eyes glared green with hate and fury, and his jaw snapped with a hollow 'chop,' as he vainly endeavored to reach me and my trembling horse. But he was worn out with hunger and struggling and loss of blood, and he soon sank exhausted to the ground."

Seton's farewell speech to the wolf was also, it seems, to the cowboys he'd taken with him. "Grand old outlaw, hero of a thousand lawless raids, in a few minutes you will be a great load of carrion. It cannot be otherwise."

He threw his lasso at Old Lobo, but Old Lobo reached up and bit the rope in half in mid-air.

Not wanting to mar the hide with a rifle shot, Seton galloped back home for new ropes, came back and tossed Lobo a stick of wood, and while Lobo's jaw closed on the chunk of wood, they lassoed him.

"Yet before the light had died from his fierce eyes, I cried, 'Stay, we will not kill him; let us take him alive to the camp.'"

They lashed his jaws shut around a stick and strapped him firmly to the back of the horse. In this final humiliation, "he never groaned, nor growled, nor turned his head. His breath came evenly as though sleeping, and his eyes were bright and clear again, but did not rest on us. Afar on the great rolling mesas they were fixed, his passing kingdom, where his famous band was now scattered. And he gazed till the pony descended the pathway into the cañon, and the rocks cut off the view.

"By traveling slowly we reached the ranch in safety, and after securing him with a collar and a strong chain, we staked him out in the pasture and removed the cords."

"I set meat and water beside him, but he paid no heed. He lay calmly on his breast, and gazed with those steadfast yellow eyes away past me down through the gateway of the cañon, over the open plains—his plains—nor moved a muscle when I touched him. When the sun went down he was still gazing fixedly across the prairie."

There's barely room or space in this tale for Seton, having shown off his catch to his fellow ranchmates, to self flagellate now.

"A lion shorn of his strength, an eagle robbed of his freedom, or a dove bereft of his mate, all die, it is said, of a broken heart; and who will aver that this grim bandit could bear the threefold brunt, heart-whole? This only I know, that when the morning dawned, he was lying there still in his position of calm repose, his body unwounded, but his spirit was gone—the old King-wolf was dead."

They took the chains and ropes from his neck and carried him into the shed where the three-footed body of Blanca remained and laid him out next to her, and one of the cattlemen remarked, "There you *would* come to her, now you are together again"—as if believing that some great order and balance had been struck, rather than a continuation of the most severe unraveling.

So 105 years later, the Turkey Creek male—possessing no Spanish surname, but instead, "Wolf #156," in the jargon of the times—was turned out onto the same-but-different land, where he and his mate had that brief month of freedom. After he attacked the dog (which had been chained to a stake), both "sides" of the West—conservationists and wolf fearers—were quick to cry "I told you so." It's hard to imagine what the star-wolf, the Turkey Creek male, thought of all that, as he, or the story of his quick but ancient passage, swirled with all else that has gone: hunting only among the stars at night now; hunting only in our imagination. As if the safest or surest way for a wolf to exist in this century is to be completely invisible; as invisible as a star in daytime, or as harmless as an old story.

So before the dust becomes too old, it is possible to go back and try to find out what kind of wolf the Turkey Creek male might have been. It's a hard question, because all along the protocol has been to not observe or establish contact with the wolves—to keep them as separate from the world of humans as possible. Still, if one hurries, a few scraps of testimony can be gleaned before the dust not of a hundred years ago, but yesterday, or last week, or last month, blows on past.

Colleen Buchanan, at the Sevilleta Refuge in New Mexico, was his keeper for the year and a half preceding his freedom. She didn't see him much, but he was her favorite, she says. All the other wolves would "just sleep" all the time, but the Turkey Creek male was very active—a very strong alpha, "a great wolf."

He had all the instincts and strengths a wild wolf needs. He was loyal and territorial. Coyotes would sometimes come in from out of the desert and sit on the other side of the fence to taunt him, and he'd run at the fence, which had an electric "hot" wire in it, but he didn't care. He'd leap up and pull the electric fence down with his teeth, trying to get past it so that he could then tear at the chain-link fence. He'd pull down five, six, seven hot wires at a time.

Had he known in his heart that one day he was going to be able to get through that fence? One can only hope, and imagine, the joy or sense of rightness he must have felt, that his struggles, his unyieldingness, had finally resulted in his freedom.

He was a great wolf. He was not a pet wolf or a zoo wolf, but an "old" wolf.

Buchanan says she doesn't like to anthropomorphize, but that he established "a very strong pair bond" with the Turkey Creek female immediately; that he "instantly became attached to her," within minutes of being introduced; that it was like "love at first sight. He followed her everywhere," she says, right from the very beginning, and they were inseparable thereafter. "They would sleep curled up as close to each other as they could," she says, "like spoons. They were just always together."

What chart of stars directed that dog, that camper, to set up in the heart of the Turkey Creek pair's territory, putting an alien canid in the heart of their country, with the Turkey Creek male's mate pregnant and expecting to whelp any day? Afterward, biologists found that the Turkey Creek male had already made territorial scrapes in the campground: that either the camper and dog—and Turkey Creek pair—had just been the victims of sheer blind bad luck, or the most awful and unchanging direction of fate.

Luck so bad that you plead for another pattern, another story, another chance.

The Turkey Creek male's death left the biologists—and not least of all the Turkey Creek female, alone in the world—in the worst quandary: what to do, if she were pregnant?

She couldn't whelp the pups and survive—couldn't stay with them, or she (as well as the pups) would starve. But she couldn't leave them and go off to hunt, or they'd die of exposure, or starve, or wander out of the den and get lost or caught and killed by almost anything.

Should the Turkey Creek female be recaptured, and sent back to captivity for another year? Or, due to her association with the dog fighter, jailed for life—having been given a month's freedom, but then having a life's worth taken away?

And what of her pups, if any—one of the cornerstones for the future of wild Mexican wolves to come; what confusion, if any—what disruption of story—would reside within their blood, having been nestled snug in the belly of their mother, who was in the belly of her den, in the belly of freedom; listening through her to the day-and-night rhythms of that place, only to then emerge from her and be back where they had started out, behind fences? To have known, in some dim way, freedom for barely a month, without having ever even seen or smelled it?

There are no neat stories in nature, no tidy closures with beginning, middle, and end; no epiphanies. There is only on-going process, continuous struggle.

There are only the old, old stories, which tend to follow, like rivers, the paths of all that has come before them, cutting back ever deeper into the past. It requires monumental power, almost unnatural power, to scribe or carve a new story in the midst and presence of such history.

The decision was made finally to capture the Turkey Creek female and bring her back to captivity. She was caught on a Sunday, and taken back to Sevilleta. The next day she gave birth. The managers at the refuge didn't go in and examine her; for eight weeks, they would avoid all contact with her to let her and her offspring remain as wild as possible, there on the other side of that fence. Only one pup survived. And it was hoped that, maybe, one day that pup would be sent back out into the world.

After it's all played out, we are only now ready to begin again.

EPILOGUE

It wasn't neat, it won't be neat. We cannot compress millions of years of evolution into the last hundred years, nor can that wildness be butted up tight against this century's wall; at best we can find spaces large enough or rich enough to accommodate it. As the Turkey Creek pack was dissolved, the other two packs cinched their movements up tight, then stopped wandering altogether and dug dens, indicating they, too, were ready to whelp. (For fear of disrupting the packs, the biologists wouldn't be able to approach the dens to count the pups; they would have to wait for the pups to mature and emerge from the den on their own, and for the pups to move toward them).

One of the wolves in the Campbell Blue pack (probably the alpha male) killed a rancher's blue heeler dog. (Defenders of Wildlife is working with the rancher to assist in the purchase and training of a new dog.) Already the release was starting to seem like some lupine soap opera. A yearling female, also from the Campbell Blue pack—Wolf #511—dispersed, seeking adolescent independence. She traveled almost seventy miles to an area northwest of the town of Showlow, Arizona. More strangeness: a twenty-one-inch tall miniature horse colt was attacked in a corral by a wolf, according to the tracks left in the dirt. It's believed that the attacker might have been this wolf. The colt's mother defended her baby and chased the wolf away, and the colt is expected to survive. (What must the wolf have thought, when she saw such a tiny horse? Did she believe she was attacking an elk calf or deer fawn? Was the wolf's blood-memory confused by the sight—wondering, perhaps, if new creatures had arisen in the world since the wolves were last free?)

Although Wolf #511's wandering behavior is normal for young wolves, the young female wouldn't have been able to find a packmate—not this first year, not on that wolfless plain—and so she was captured and taken back to Sevilleta. Despite her travels she was in excellent health and was "acting much wilder than before her release into the wild," said Colleen Buchanan. Perhaps she'll be a candidate for next year's release, or the next year's.

Around the same time, a second female, a two-year old, had left the big Hawk's Nest pack: Wolf #494. (Where do they get these numbers? What gap exists in the biologists' heart between calling a thing by a number, and then watching that thing strike out for independence and travel seventy miles alone, into the future? You can bet that after such an incident they start thinking not in numbers, but in nouns and verbs, adjectives, *story*).

The second young female—call her #494 as we must, for documentary's sake—appeared to have left the Hawk's Nest pack in response to the alpha female's denning.

This young female began hanging out around the town of Alpine, Arizona (not far from where Jerry Scoville had his run-in with the pistol-waving countryman).

As had been the case with the earlier dispersing young female, this wolf wouldn't have been able to find a mate, or even a hunting partner. Additionally, "her continued presence in the area of human settlement was undesirable," according to the USF&WS, so she too was captured and taken back to Sevilleta.

(One of Sevilleta's volunteer caretakers, Sheila Hebst, reported that when the two back-to-back recaptured females were placed in the same pen, it generated great interest and excitement among the other wolves and that all four male wolves at a near-by pen were "standing on their hind legs against the fence . . . trying to get a look.")

So now they were down to seven. As Robinson Jeffers wrote, the wolf's tooth has whittled the fleet limbs of the antelope, but now there are hundreds of millions of humans, and our activities are whittling down these last hundred-plus wolves into some strange new blade's edge—some new and shifting but honed thing, almost fragile in its final integrity, the outcome of which neither the land nor the wolves nor ourselves are yet aware.

Carving down—below *what was*, deep and far into *what is to come*.

From eleven wild wolves to seven. Except that it wasn't seven any more. Presumably, hopefully, there were wolf pups writhing like possibility beneath the ground this spring and summer: fattening on mother's milk, then chewing elk haunches with pin teeth, and cracking deer bones with little jaws; wrestling and growling and playing as if none of what has already happened—in any century—matters. As if there is nothing but future. As if the past is no anchor, is no boundary to their territory. *Living*.

By June the biologists were waiting for the elk calving season to start, and for the social pressures of denning season to wane a bit. A 420-acre fire burned across the Campbell Blue pack's territory, as if welcoming the wolves.

The Hawk's Nest pack was believed to have birthed pups, but it appears that none survived, because the pack has left its den and is hunting again.

Both packs began chasing and catching elk calves, plenty of free and easy meat, and it's hoped there might be a lull in the drama. The Hawk's Nest pack was observed chasing and "testing" cattle that wandered into their territory; no depredations occurred, however. Another young female—Wolf #493—from the Hawk's Nest pack dispersed and wandered to the western edges of the recovery area, where she tried to attack a calf, but the rancher successfully scared the wolf away. Next, she went to a developed campground, for reasons unknown, but probably having to do with food. How hard it must be to hunt alone.

When she wouldn't leave the campgrounds, biologists trapped her in a soft-catch foothold trap—she was uninjured—and returned her to her old haunts, to the circumscribed boundaries where the biologists wanted her to stay.

Yet another wolf from the Hawk's Nest pack, a young male by the name of #531, had dispersed around this same period over onto the White Mountain Apache Reservation, but he returned, so that for the time being, the Hawk's Nest Five were all reunited, and once more within the borders of the area that the recovery plan had mapped for them.

The pup that had survived from the Turkey Creek tragedy—conceived in semi-captivity, carried in its mother's womb into the wild, but then born in full captivity—died; the cause of death could not be determined.

They were all just hanging on: less than hanging on—
dwindling, scrambling, wandering.

The Campbell Blue pair seemed, for the moment, to be
operating with the most security, though even they, too, were
having a tough time of it. In June, the female took down an elk
calf with the help of her mate, but the calf's bawls had brought
the mother elk storming to the rescue; the cow elk stomped on
the Campbell Blue female good, so that she had to crawl off,
dragging her hind legs.

Nonetheless, the Campbell Blue female continued to
make forays with the male—they were both observed fighting a
pair of coyotes over a freshly killed elk calf—but the biologists
weren't sure she'd be able to survive, and for a while, as she con-
valesced, they went back to feeding her (and her mate) frozen
deer and elk carcasses.

The hope was that the supplemental feeding would speed
the healing of her injury; and perhaps it worked, because two
weeks later (though still limping), she participated with the male
in an attack on a cow elk, which they wounded and then chased
to bay in a stock tank.

The temperature down in Tempe that week climbed to
116 degrees; 120 in Bullhead City, 130 in Death Valley, with
summer still building.

The two Campbell Blue wolves must have watched that
hurt elk out in the water: pacing, waiting, resting. Watching.
Carving their way back into time, and place, and history.

Three days later, biologists received yet another surprise.
The Campbell Blue pair—the injured female and her mate—

were sighted with a single pup, which they must have moved to a hiding spot back when the biologists were examining the various dens a month earlier.

While the parents were taking care of their pup, the cow elk in the stock tank finally escaped—the yaw, the pitch and rise of nature—life seeping through the cracks like sand running between clasped fingers. But the next day, the Campbell Blue pair caught another elk and killed it.

Their pup is the first Mexican wolf known to be born in the wild in this country in over fifty years, and it is being raised on wild elk meat. He's all they've got, all we've got, and the team members are very happy. Even if something ultimately happens to the pup, says Wendy Brown, the first year can now be considered a success at least that far: the pack successfully gave birth to a pup in the wild.

The hot new world simmers and boils below. It's cooler, up in the mountains. Hunting season's coming, for our own species. The snow will come again. Will these wolves still be in the world then? Will they still exist in the wild, or will they have been brought back to captivity? If they are still out in the wild, will they move lower—will they migrate with the changing season—or will they remain in their mountain stronghold?

Events—awkward, unmanageable—will continue to happen: surprise after surprise, setbacks and triumphs. We mustn't underestimate the wolves' force: their ability to live hugely in the world.

They are going to seek their old borders, old territories. They are going to chase elk, cross boundaries, make mistakes, and learn, or not learn, this new world. Even as it is time for this book to be bound and shipped, strange and unpredictable things will be taking place.

I remember back when the Round River students and other volunteers were working on the pens at Turner's Ladder Ranch. I remember how in the heat of the day, I had the sun-struck notion of burying some artifact, some tangible physical object, deep into the cement foundation beneath the stone wall where the workers were laboring, and above which the wolves would be housed.

That time, and this story—the last few years preceding the wolves' release—have already passed, while the wolves are still traveling, coming and going, continuing to make their own stories in layers atop our stories, which rest in turn in layers atop their stories, which rest atop how the land was, back then. . . .

The hills are moving with the wolves again. The mountains are moving with rhythms we have not seen in a long, long time. After having been still—like a slow pause—the forests are alive with wolves again. The yelps and yips from a single pup issue forth nightly from a hole in the ground—the den in the mountains beneath starry skies.

There is no map of the future. We can only watch and listen, and hope to learn from the past, as well as from the present, that which we did not learn the first time.